Hack witl

An editor's back stories of SA news

GASANT ABARDER

Published by BestRed, an imprint of HSRC Press
Private Bag X9182, Cape Town, 8000, South Africa
www.bestred.co.za

First published 2020

ISBN (soft cover) 978-1-928246-38-1

© 2020 Human Sciences Research Council

The views expressed in this publication are those of the author. They do not necessarily reflect the views or policies of the Human Sciences Research Council (the Council) or indicate that the Council endorses the views of the author. In quoting from this publication, readers are advised to attribute the source of the information to the author and not to the Council.

The publishers have no responsibility for the continued existence or accuracy of URLs for external or third-party Internet websites referred to in this book and do not guarantee that any content on such websites is, or will remain, accurate or appropriate.

Copy-edited by Juliet Gillies
Index by Jennifer Stern
Typeset by Karen Lilje
Cover design by Malick Abarder
Cover illustration by Dayaan Abarder
Printed by Capitil Press, Cape Town, Sout Africa

Distributed in Africa by Blue Weaver
Tel: +27 (021) 701 4477; Fax Local: (021) 701 7302
www.blueweaver.co.za

Distributed in Europe and the United Kingdom by Eurospan Distribution Services (EDS)
Tel: +44 (0) 17 6760 4972; Fax: +44 (0) 17 6760 1640
www.eurospanbookstore.com

Distributed in North America by Lynne Rienner Publishers, Inc.
Tel: +1 303-444-6684; Fax: 303-444-0824; Email: cservice@rienner.com
www.rienner.com

Suggested citation: Gasant Abarder (2020) *Hack with a grenade: An editor's back stories of SA news*. Cape Town: BestRed

Contents

Foreword

In an ever-changing world, especially with the print media houses having to deal with the additional challenge of online media and social media in the past decade, print media has had to adapt and become more innovative in working to keep the newspapers alive.

I have always had the greatest respect for the media as the fourth estate, with its integral role of keeping government and politicians accountable and, as importantly, telling the stories of the people of our cities to make sure their stories reach the powers that be.

Indeed, journalism is more than just about record keeping – that's the job of an archive. Journalism is about education, awareness, advocacy and helping to bring about change.

I have often heard journalists say that they went into the field to be a voice for the voiceless and to help change people's lives by telling their stories and effecting change, so that those who need to bring about change do so, and are held accountable.

As an activist and politician, my respect for journalists goes beyond the role they play in holding government to account. During the late 1990s when I exposed the Arms Deal, I relied on the media to get the stories out – and in doing so, they saved my life. Working with the media helped to ensure that those who had put a target on me would not be safe coming after me, as many more people knew about the Arms Deal saga.

When one talks about the print media in Cape Town, the *Cape Argus* and *Cape Times* are the key players. These papers have always been important to the people of Cape Town.

Beyond the usual politics, crime stories and big exposés, there was indeed a fundamental shift that happened during the time of Gasant Abarder's editorship. One such example that stands out was during the #FeesMustFall protests. #FeesMustFall was emotionally and politically charged, and Gasant displayed great courage in taking students into his confidence and handing students the reins as co-editors of the paper at one stage. Some would say this was a risky move, but it was courageous, brilliant and an innovative way of telling this story by having the students at the centre of these protests write their own stories, and jointly edit the paper with Gasant and his team. This was 'giving the community a voice' in action. By giving students a space, they were able to put their Struggle perspective forward.

The media landscape was changing and continues to change at a rapid pace. While media houses push to stay ahead of the digital curve or catch up with it, there are still residents who have been lifelong newspaper subscribers, who appreciate and need the 'Argie' in their hands every day.

Yes, we consume most of our news online and we are being updated by the second through online news sites, Facebook and Twitter, but the case for newspapers is still strong. The only thing is that, like with all things, we cannot stick to the same methodology of planning or the same way of doing things.

One particularly refreshing feature was that of Danny Oosthuizen, a homeless man from Cape Town. The story of the homeless in Cape Town is a sad and complex one. On the one hand, residents call for the government to do something and to 'clean' the streets, while on the other hand, some of the homeless people have nowhere to go. The streets are their escape from homes of pain, abuse and many other things, which those of us with normal lives, homes and loving families would probably never be able to comprehend. Homelessness is also a global problem and an issue that many governments across the world grapple with. Like with many other issues, Cape Town is no different on this score.

The start of Danny's column added a whole new layer to the 'giving a voice to the voiceless' approach. It added a whole new layer to understanding the battles and issues that the homeless face. I would hope that it made readers see homeless people as human beings, thinkers, smart people and people with aspirations who want better, but who do not have the support they require from society to get them back on track.

Danny's columns were an eye-opener to many, as he held government and other entities to account. He advocated for all street people, he joked, he was happy and sad, and he bared his mind and soul in those columns.

Sadly, Danny passed away in 2019; but the opportunity he was given by Gasant to publish a weekly column in the *Cape Argus* is one I am sure made a meaningful impact on Danny's life during his last years. This, along with the regular columns by Gasant, took the newspaper back to the days of reporting and reflecting life across the whole of Cape Town in a more holistic way. It went beyond just reporting on what was happening in the City Council chambers, the Provincial Legislature, Parliament, the business boardrooms, the sports fields and around press conference tables. Many of the innovative changes Gasant and his team brought about were about engaging on a deeper level with those who made the news, and refreshingly moving away from the hit-and-run type of reporting.

To my mind, Danny's column broke many stereotypes and prejudices that people had about homeless people. At least I hope it did. I hope that it brought forward some more humanity and compassion for our fellow human beings who are not able to go home or really have no home.

Indeed, the media plays an important role in shaping how people think, and how their psyche develops.

During his time as editor of the *Cape Times* and *Cape Argus*, I was the Mayor of Cape Town and at the helm of a city where many things were changing, but many things remained the same. The media was an important partner and I always tried to be as accessible as possible. Many journalists knew that I was accessible, but not many used that open door policy to their full advantage. Gasant stands out as one editor who wouldn't hesitate to pick up the phone and call for clarity or for an interview during difficult times. He went beyond how many reporters were reporting on City of Cape Town matters, and my political battle during 2017 and 2018, and had difficult but necessary conversations with me. He took the time to delve into issues on a deeper level and reflect the issues in a balanced and fair manner.

I always say that I do not fight with people in charge of thousands of barrels of ink, so no matter how the *Cape Times* and *Cape Argus* reported on matters in the City of Cape Town or on me as a politician, I had respect for them, as they were never afraid to pick up the phone and call me and use the access which I made available to everyone.

The introduction of tabloid newspapers in the late 2000s was also a very important step for the media landscape in Cape Town, and an especially necessary news source for the people of the Cape Flats. With the establishment of the *Daily Voice*, the real stories of the people of the Cape Flats and our townships really came to the fore, telling of the life and struggles of the often-forgotten part of the Cape Town population. While the pages of the tabloids were filled with crime and gangsterism, this was the life on the Cape Flats; but at the other end of this spectrum, the tabloids gave a glimpse into all the strange and hilarious happenings on the Cape Flats.

It provided people with news about what was happening in communities like Bontehuewel, Manenberg, Ocean View, Gugulethu and Khayelistha, to name a few. And when a young child from a poor community went missing or was a victim of a crime, the story received the same prominence that usually goes with something happening to a child from an affluent part of Cape Town.

For a mere R2 (at one stage), the people of the Cape Flats could get their news fix in a way that they understood it. No matter what some may think of tabloids, they informed and educated the people who would not necessarily buy, or could not afford, a *Cape Times* or *Cape Argus*.

With the rise of tabloids, people's interest in news grew. I am sure many of us have heard people say: 'Did you read that story in the *Voice* today?' That is how the majority of residents on the Cape Flats received their news and where many important stories were told. In fact, many times, residents trusted the tabloids more than the other newspapers. From the scoops, to the humour, to the important stories of the day, the tabloids certainly played an important role in Cape Town, and in how residents were informed and educated.

During his tenure as editor of the *Cape Times* and *Cape Argus*, there were many major Cape Town stories that Gasant and his team delved deeper into. Two examples are the painful story of Zephany Nurse and the heartbreak of District Six – marred by the slow pace of restitution and the return of the people to this place, which was once a beacon of inclusivity.

This book will provide readers with greater insight into the behind-the-scenes working of two of Cape Town's biggest newspapers. Both these papers have an illustrious history in our city and are renowned for their journalism. Indeed, the time of Gasant's editorship was one of the key periods in the history and evolution of these newspapers and the media industry at large.

It takes courage, conviction and determination to change the way journalists report – to go beyond the usual, and to do so in no more than 450 words. Honestly, not much can be said in that many words, and so exploring new ideas and implementing them did these newspapers a great deal of good. More importantly, it did a great deal of good in doing its job of informing and educating the masses.

It is my hope that, as our country continues to go through massive changes, as we stand at a crossroads, as we work to strengthen our democracy, more journalists will have the courage to disrupt the old way of thinking and doing things. In doing things differently and responsibly, we will serve our fellow South Africans better.

Long may the spirit and work of the fourth estate continue.

Patricia de Lille
Minister of Public Works and Infrastructure

Preface

My timing sucks. I decided to write a book about the written word – about newspaper journalism to be precise – and have it published when both books and newspapers are under threat. Perhaps this is what makes this book poignant, as each medium begins to reimagine itself in the new normal brought about by COVID-19.

The genesis of this book, however, began years ago. In 2011, I wrote a few chapters for a manuscript I provisionally titled, *Tabloid Junkie*. Parts of Chapter 1 of this book were written then, and it took the wizardry of an IT guru to rescue those first rough drafts from the hard drive of a laptop that suddenly packed up.

I had forgotten about *Tabloid Junkie* when I first arrived at the offices of HSRC Press at the behest of my good friend Vernon Joshua, a publishing veteran who is now retired. He introduced me to publishing director Jeremy Wightman and commissioning editor Mthunzi Nxawe. Initially, I had a very different book in mind and wanted to compile a collection of profiles I had written for the *Cape Argus* into a book. But Jeremy and Mthunzi told me the hard truth, i.e. that a book like that would never work. I am so glad I listened to them.

They encouraged me to use the profiles as the raw material for this book. But they wanted to hear my voice as the storyteller. I am indebted to them for their foresight, and for not allowing me to go down rabbit holes. I am grateful to Vernon, Jeremy and Mthunzi for encouraging me to tell a South African story through the eyes of a newspaper editor – the back stories that make newsrooms and the people of our beautiful country tick.

I am immensely grateful to my wife, Laylaa Abarder, without whom I may still have been sitting with an incomplete manuscript. She taught me to stop saying, 'One day when I'm retired and the bond is paid up...' and instead say, 'Today is day one'. I love you and our children from The Loud House, Ziyaad, Kehara, Misha and Ariana. As I forge a new path as a corporate media professional, I want to thank my current boss and self-appointed life coach, Patricia Lawrence, Director of Institutional Advancement at the University of the Western Cape, for giving me the freedom to experiment, make mistakes and learn. The small team of media people at the university are among the best I've had the privilege to work with.

I owe a great debt of gratitude too to my best friends, The Chicken Licken Boys, for keeping me honest. Also to my parents for allowing me to chase my dream of being a journalist, despite their misgivings. When we were growing up, my dad complained that my brother – his one son – 'drew poppentjies (a Cape Flats reference to cartoons) and the other one told stories'. Look at us now, Dad! This book cover is a childhood pact between my eldest brother, Malick Abarder, and me, with finished artwork by his son, Dayaan Abarder.

In the media world, no one teaches you to be a leader. Each of my peers and mentors gave a little of themselves and their wisdom along my journey. Roger Friedman, Benny Gool, Jimi Matthews, Shahied Teladia, Moegsien Williams, Lucky Tsolo, Ayesha Ismail, Karl Brophy, Mondli Makhanya, Kevin Ritchie, Robyn Leary, Alan Dunn, Yunus Kemp, Lutfia Vayej, Mark Keohane, Lance Witten, Sandy Naude, Lyntina Aimes, Ray Joseph, Natasha Joseph, Jade Otto and my many former colleagues in various newsrooms around the country: thank you for inspiring me.

The greatest gift an editor can give a journalist – whether a copy sub, field reporter, photographer or layout designer – is trusting them. It is not the space to micromanage, but to trust all of the parts of the sum to make a whole. It is most rewarding when someone you've led becomes a leader.

I thank the Almighty for giving me the gift of storytelling, without which I may have been completely useless to the world. Storytelling is the only skill I know. It is a craft I am dedicated to, it is a craft I treasure, and it is a craft that we must pass to the next generation.

Introduction

'Right, you've got the grenade. Don't fuck it up!'

With those parting words, I was left in charge of the biggest, raciest tabloid newspaper South Africa would ever see – complete with a Page 3 girl.

The editor was leaving the running of the *Daily Voice* in my hands while he was away on business for a week or two. Would you trust a hack (a term in the media world for a reckless journalist) with a grenade? No, I didn't think so. Sooner or later the pin would be pulled out; limbs would be severed; blood would splatter. Worst case scenario? Death.

Yet there I was. A 27-year-old left with the ultimate responsibility of running a daily tabloid newspaper, and ensuring that no one ended up in jail or was sued – least of all me. I had to be extra careful on these occasions, because the *Daily Voice* was constantly pushing the envelope in the spirit of tabloid journalism.

For the next 15 years, in senior editorial roles and ultimately as editor of two of South Africa's oldest daily newspapers, I carried this personal mantra with me and constantly reminded myself: 'I've got the grenade now. I dare not fuck this up.'

As I graduated to editor of newspapers that a tabloid hack on London's Fleet Street would refer to as 'the unpopulars' – a derogatory term for the so-called respectable broadsheet papers – the hack became thicker-skinned and more cynical. All the while, the grenade became more powerful and explosive.

'Hack with a grenade' is a metaphor for the burden of responsibility all editors should feel when they put a newspaper to bed. It should keep you up at night; make you sweat; make you pray that the phone call that just woke you up in the middle of the night, hours after the paper had rolled off the presses, isn't the one that goes, 'Boss, we got it horribly wrong. We're going to have to do damage control in the morning.'

In a racially charged world, in which we are still grappling with the simple idea that #BlackLivesMatter, the media carries the grenade. The carrier of the grenade holds the burden of responsibility. The media sits on the powder keg, and pulling the pin can cause a charged environment to become explosive.

It is incredibly sobering that, in this context, when the world needs them the most, newspapers are fighting for their survival. Newspapers have been caught in a schizophrenic existence of dipping their toes in the digital space while not being able to remain true to the fine tradition of publishing credible news. During my own journey as a newspaper editor, I straddled these worlds often. There was a fine line between an absolute clanger of a front page, influenced heavily by the chattering classes on social media, and a masterstroke of a front page. I was living a frenetic life from one front page to the next.

Decades ago, when the first newspapers rolled off the presses, they were the preserve of notices, announcements and advertisements. They were peculiar in that they recorded the peculiarities of the day almost matter-of-factly – a first draft of history – that when read decades later would be – at times – almost offensive, if not downright hilarious, were the events often not so tragic.

In *Paging Through History – 150 Years with the Cape Argus, 1857 – 2007*, the author, Michael Morris, wrote in my autographed copy: 'In the first days of January 1857, the frontier crisis was one of the major news reports carried in the Colony's newest newspaper.

'The founding edition of the *Cape Argus*, the first issues of which came off Saul Solomon's modern steam press at 63 Longmarket Street in the early hours of 3 January, alerted readers to the risk of a new war in the east.

'"The most experienced men on the frontier," a correspondent in Aberdeen wrote, "believe that it is inevitable."

'This eternal anticipation of conflict would be the recurring theme of much of the next century and a half of liberal journalism in an emerging state that repeatedly delayed confronting the political and moral challenge of citizenship.

'But in 1857 – even if the doings of Flaubert and Verdi, of Marx and Darwin, the jurists and gangsters of America or the oil pioneers of Romania were unreported or unheard of in provincial Cape Town – the city's self-image was probably being more markedly fashioned by its widening access to a heady international cosmos.

'Global mercantilism was on resplendent display in Table Bay on 3 January, where no fewer than 40 vessels rode at anchor, ships, barques, barquentines, brigs, brigantines, schooners and a steamer from, among other places, London, Batavia, Copenhagen, Rio de Janeiro, Newcastle, Hamburg, Glasgow, Rotterdam, Trinidad, Bremen, Mauritius and Gothenburg.'

(Gosh, I wish I could write like Michael Morris!)

Exactly two years after the 150th anniversary of the *Cape Argus*, the grenade was entrusted to this hack. Gasant Abarder, descendant of slaves perhaps anchored in Table Bay on one of those very vessels on 3 January 1857, became the youngest editor of this prestigious newspaper at just 31 years old. I would have buckled under the weight of responsibility were it not for the confidence of my youth, and the unparalleled support of journalists like Michael Morris, Michael Doman and Leon Müller.

I was four years ahead of the curve I had set myself. My plan had been to become an editor of a mainstream newspaper by the time I was 35. I had always wanted to be a journalist – since I was just six years old, and there was a murder at the last house in our cul de sac in Mitchells Plain on the Cape Flats. I remember the flashing press cameras. As I grew up, I flirted with other careers. Marketing? Law? Attractive, but somehow, I would always go back to that moment in 1984 at the end of the cul de sac. I had a romantic notion about journalism and it had to be newspapers.

(Besides, I could tell one helluva story. But I couldn't count or add. It is said that there are three types of journalists: those who can count and those who can't!)

There is something about the feel of newsprint, the ink transferring onto your fingers as you page through the paper, the smell and the pinch factor of an edition that is fatter-than-usual. There is nothing like breaking a story in a newspaper when you've invested time and resources into that story.

Never in my wildest dreams, though, did I imagine becoming editor of the newspaper I read while growing up. My hometown paper. As the co-founders, Bryan Henry Darnell and Richard William Murray imagined it, the *Cape Argus* would be welcomed into the merchant's office and family home alike – a champion of good causes and non-partisan, but forthright.

I was described as a bolt from the blue; the tabloid hack who had come good and was now editor of an 'unpopular' title. Or had he? I was determined to show I was more than just a one-trick-pony and my experience in TV journalism would stand me in good stead. I needed to fill some big shoes to carry on the legacy of a fine newspaper. Now I needed to advance the newspaper's founding credo that carried it through times of conflict like world wars, and our transition from a colony, to apartheid state, and on to democracy.

I was fortunate in being appointed editor of the *Cape Times* as well – another great institution of my hometown. Given a choice though, the *Cape Argus* will always be my first love. It was there that I cut my teeth as an editor, and it was there that I tried to re-imagine newspapers in the mould of Darnell and Murray.

How times changed though. In 2009, TV and radio news were no longer even a threat. Long gone too were the days that newspapers, like the grand old lady, *Argus*, were newspapers of record. Yet there we were, still reporting yesterday's news when Twitter, Facebook and other social media and online platforms were breaking the news at a rate traditional media just couldn't live with.

In another lifetime, it seemed, but which was just 12 years earlier, I was given a device that looked like a cordless telephone. It had letters on the number pad, and I was told to file my story on it. Then I asked, as a 19-year-old intern at *The Star* newspaper in Johannesburg, if I should write the story using the letters on the number pad. It evoked hearty laughter in the newsroom. That day I had my very first front-page lead about Max, the crime-fighting gorilla who had mauled a burglar who had jumped into his enclosure at the Joburg Zoo. Max suffered a bullet wound but was named SA Crime Fighter of 1997. I filed the story via a dictate to the newsroom editorial assistant, using what was my first experience with a cellphone.

(As it later turned out, the letters were on that number pad for good reason, and I was onto something. SMSs were in fact later used to file stories from a scene.)

As the race to be first became the commodity of news, the rule book was among the first to be tossed out of the window. The next casualty was ethics. Later, quality began suffering too, as newsrooms shrunk to a quarter of their size. Newspapers, in particular, suffered hefty blows, like a heavyweight in the final rounds of a bout refusing to throw in the towel. Somehow, hope remained that the fighter would make a comeback and deliver a knockout blow in the final round.

To put it in perspective: when I was first appointed editor of the *Cape Argus* in 2009, there were 57 staff. When I left mainstream media in 2018, there were exactly 10 staff at the *Cape Argus* – including the editor. With reduced budgets, editors were doing the best they could in an ever-changing media landscape. The payroll budget was chopped and straight-out-of-varsity journos were hired to do the work that Morris, Doman and Müller used to do.

Don't get me wrong. I am in awe of the modern journalist. If sent out to the field today I would probably run for the hills. These young people are multi-skilled. They can't afford to be a specialist or to label themselves as a TV, radio or newspaper journalist. These days a journalist working at a paper is often expected to write two to three stories a day. The storytelling happens not just in the newspaper. These young journalists are also expected to file a breaking online story, post on social media, shoot or edit or narrate a video and provide on-the-spot opinion and analysis. And they get paid less!

In a newsroom with a Morris, Doman or Müller though, I could still tell yesterday's story. That was because, even though the news had broken on another platform the day before, these greybeards – an affectionate term for the rare species that is a senior journalist – would push the story further the following day. Despite the rigours of a deadline-driven daily newspaper, the newspaper would provide depth, analysis and meaning – all gloriously written with context and attention to detail so that the readers could pore over the story the following day.

But when there is no time, you are a rookie, and when you look up and there are no mentors to turn to, your story is going to say the same thing that Twitter said yesterday. Because of the shrinking newsroom syndrome, editors are cutting corners and the result is that the purveyors of credible news are losing their very currency because of the desire for quick-wins, viral traffic to websites and the most clickable content.

I used to laugh at the phrase 'juniorisation of newsrooms'. It is a fallacy, because by their nature, journalists set themselves apart from citizen content producers because they follow a code. It is a code or an order that separates the wheat from the chaff. This responsibility holds true for the most junior journalist right up to the editor-in-chief. The public is meant to first corroborate information by testing what they read, hear or see on one of their social media platforms or online against a credible news source. But in the age of the information superhighway, we are all too keen to believe whatever pops up on our smartphone screens. As consumers of news, we are part of the blurring of the line between what is credible and what is fiction.

The chance for newspapers to land a sucker punch and claim their space never arrived. That is not to say they never had a chance. Somewhere in Round 6 of the bout (in the mid-1990s) they had a chance to put a punch combo together and cement themselves as the heavyweight champs of the media world. But the going was too good. Advertisers were throwing money at newspapers like there was no tomorrow. Like Kodak and camera film, newspapers were under the illusion that the day would never arrive that paper and ink would be too expensive.

That day is upon us and, regrettably, newspapers are still writing yesterday's story. There was no greater reality check than when the first major disruptor of the 21st Century, COVID-19, arrived. If newspapers were not already on an intravenous drip by the winter of 2020, this new silent, invisible and indiscriminate killer was about to put it on a life support machine. Just weeks into the global pandemic, the scribes were writing the obituaries as newspaper after newspaper was killed off.

The newspapers left standing are the ones that had owners who understood their roles. Newspapers that continue to grow their circulation, like the New York Times and the Washington Post, have owners who leave the business of producing great papers to the professionals. They stay away from the newsrooms they own. Their relationship, as it should be, is like church and state. The two never mix. Never. These owners create the environment in which newspapers thrive, and a space conducive to investigating scandals in the great tradition of newspapering like no other medium can. Whether they get a return on investment is not really as important as the good they do for democracy.

The great scandals of the 20th century were all broken by newspapers. They took painstaking investigation in many cases and significant resources. These exclusive investigations were usually followed up by the TV and radio station news teams.

Now, without lifting a finger, the Googles and Facebooks of this world literally own the media landscape and the lion's share of global media advertising. Because they have the reach, they can aggregate the best news at zero cost to themselves while milking a steady income stream from advertising.

The ad execs who were laughing back in the '90s aren't laughing anymore. They laughed when Gumtree was launched, when they had an opportunity to turn the money-spinners that were the classified sections or smalls of newspapers into a mass online business. Now Gumtree is having the last laugh.

When they were making money hand-over-fist in those heady days, the newspaper bosses and owners weren't investing in journalism. Instead, they treated it no differently to the way the owner of a supermarket chain treats revenues and profits. Except, the owners of supermarket chains mostly had the foresight to change the way they did business, and are now far more responsive to their customers' needs. Unfortunately, the same cannot be said, for the most part, for how newspapers have treated their customers.

The result is a poorer democracy, thanks to the demise of these institutions that form part of the fourth estate – the checks and balances that hold power to account. In its place is the noise and the race to be first to the news, often at the expense of accuracy, fairness, balance and reason.

What makes newspapers unique as a medium is that, in these confusing times when audiences have to discern between fact and fiction, newspapers have the potential to offer a conversation. They can provide the step back we all need to introspect. They have the potential to be an advocate for change. They can help inform and shape public opinion.

But most of all, the defusing of the powder keg and the burden of responsibility rests on newspapers – they need to be the sobering voice of reason. They need to be measured and careful about every word and its meaning in any given edition. They need to sweat over every story written, and to be anxious when deadlines come and go.

When the world is falling apart around us, it is up to the holder of the grenade, aka the newspaper editor, to find the voices of reason and bring the temperature down in a highly charged environment. It is the duty of the editor to make sense of all the noise around an event. The editor is meant to be measured when the alternative – of pulling the pin of the grenade and setting off chaos, by chasing big newspaper sales and being irresponsible – is too ghastly to contemplate.

Fortunately, the journalism schools around the world are going back to basics. The rules apply whether you're a blogger, vlogger, newspaper journalist, TV reporter or radio correspondent, and are what sets you apart from the noise. Being cautious means your brand and your currency of credibility is far more important than being the first to break the news and then having to back-pedal later. It is the ability to separate fact from fiction. It is the ability to draw on the principles of responsible reporting and not be tempted to resorting to clickbait.

In 2017, I was lucky enough to go back to journalism school to complete my journalism degree – 20 years in the making. I was pleased to see that my majors were basic research, media ethics and newsroom leadership. The ethics course had an entire module on fake news. I learnt that there are different categories of misinformation that were lumped together under the catch-all phrase 'fake news' that US president Donald Trump loves to use to cast doubt when he paints himself into a corner.

In fact, some of Trump's utterances are probably the best examples of fake news. In truth, fake news is the deliberate creation and dissemination of untrue content that is designed to mislead audiences for financial or other gain.

The other category of misinformation is propaganda. Propaganda is dangerous because it is easy to have the ear of an inexperienced journalist when the yarn you're spinning is compelling. Propaganda is spread by those who intend to further an agenda using the media.

Dis-information is the spreading of untested statements that is caused by negligence on the part of the person spreading the news.

It is often not malicious, but that is not a good enough defence in a court of law, and the consequences of dis-information can often be disastrous, and can even ruin reputations.

Playing by the rules doesn't inhibit a journalist from being a great storyteller. But in order to bend the rules and use new devices to tell a story and draw in new audiences, we need to know the rules. The stories we tell need to be beyond reproach – whether we're telling them in a newspaper or on a social media platform. Every time we go to print, each time we hit that tweet button or when we do a live crossing, we are holding a grenade.

As COVID-19 rattled a global newspaper industry that was already under pressure, we saw pay cuts and jobs losses that were quickly followed by the closure of several newspaper titles. In all this doom and gloom, it has been asked whether there is a space or a future for newspapers. The answer is yes. But it is a long play. There is no silver bullet. It is a marathon, not a sprint, and it requires courage, determination and innovation from both editors and owners. And it requires consumers of news to be more discerning about their choices.

For an impressive period of time in the early 2000s, the owners of the London *Evening Standard* were able to turn the fortunes of an ailing newspaper around. If newspapers have it tough, evening papers (the category into which the *Cape Argus* coincidentally falls) were on a hiding to nothing. The news cycle passes them by as they try and scramble amid the scraps for a fresh angle after the morning papers have cleaned up.

But the owners of the *Evening Standard* did something very ballsy by dropping the cover charge and making it a free paper for the hundreds of thousands of train commuters going home from central London every evening. Imagine what a set of guaranteed eyeballs on each of the 600 000 copies of the paper you hand out at train stations in the CBD each evening meant to an advertiser? The fortunes of a newspaper on its deathbed were turned around in a matter of months. The profits pouring in were re-invested into a quality newspaper, and it became a refreshing read for the people of London in the way it celebrated the city, its culture, the arts and its people.

Further north, the *Liverpool Echo* was experiencing its own renaissance. The city had outgrown the hometown paper. It had become a modern metropolis of a harbour city, but the paper was still stuck in a time warp from 30 years ago, feeding the readership a diet of crime. The editorial executives took a leap of faith and decided that a stabbing in an alley would be confined to a web story, and the newspaper would be used as a celebration of all that Liverpool is – warts and all.

This is not to say that these two legacy newspaper titles started dealing in sunshine journalism as a currency. On the contrary, the newspapers became more relevant as they focused their resources on solutions-based journalism that celebrated social change and held power to account. These newspapers could not compete head on with social media, but they could give Londoners and Liverpudlians publications they could feel proud of, and which they felt they owned. They became newspapers that spoke to the aspirations and ambitions of the people of these cities as they grew and developed.

Sound familiar? Well, that was exactly what the *Daily Voice* tried to achieve with a new newspaper reader from the Cape Flats – the previously ignored readers, from the streets where I grew up, who also dreamt of a better life for the children they raised.

It also sounds familiar to me because it is exactly what Darnell and Murray had imagined the *Cape Argus* could be.

Very few people have the opportunity to be the editor of the same newspaper for two separate stints and I may be the first in the long history of the *Cape Argus*. My first stint (from 2009 to 2013) was very much a steep learning curve and I was content to play it straight and stick to the rules. But when I fortunately had the opportunity to be editor of this great publication for a second time (between 2015 and 2017), I thought long and hard about the legacy of Darnell and Murray. I thought about the editors who had gone before me, like the late Shaun Johnson, Andrew Drysdale and Moegsien Williams. I thought about the media landscape and why, with the sparse resources at my disposal, it was a bad idea to cover yesterday's news.

While I was determined to play by the rule book, it was time to be brave. It was time to innovate and be adventurous. If I didn't have the resources at my disposal, I would focus on the strength of newspapers: storytelling. I was now an active editor. I had to be. It was a very junior newsroom, and the young journalists needed me to roll up my sleeves and take them on a journey with me. Those who grew up with me before were now my elder statesmen and women.

The hack with the grenade was back. But now the hack had learnt a few new tricks and had sharpened his pencil. And the pin in the grenade was firmly intact.

Yes, we would embrace digital and social media. But they would be tools in our repertoire. I wasn't going to allow the tail (digital) to wag the dog (print). The newspaper was the premium platform that trumped all else. The digital and social media platforms were merely brand extensions.

The idea to change the way the *Cape Argus* did things was premised on a few simple principles. We couldn't compete with the internet and social media so, we had to break the stories online and on social media, so that we could retain brand recognition on these platforms while keeping our credibility intact. If it meant not being first then, damn it, we were going to be right every time. Every example of credibility displayed went straight to the bank in the mind of the reader.

So, if we told the news of the day on our brand extension platforms instead of the actual paper, what the heck were we putting in the paper? That was where the fun would be had. We would stop hunting with the pack in print. We would hunt with the pack on digital and social media platforms but push our own agenda in the printed newspaper.

I thought about Darnell and Murray. What would they do? What would an innovative editor like Shaun Johnson do? I had the challenge of sticking to the traditions built on decades of values that made the *Cape Argus* the paper it was while presenting a fresh enough face to make it withstand the challenges of a changing world.

And I did it. While others went right, I went left. In the storytelling, we experimented by giving newsmakers the space to tell their own authentic stories, sharing the space with the reports about the news they were involved in. We offered more opinion and analysis in the news pages to provide sense, analysis and meaning for the reader. When we had a big exclusive, I wouldn't trust conventional wisdom and I would break it live with a video interview on one of our platforms. The following day, the newspaper would offer a longer, more carefully crafted read that kept the reader engrossed. To my mind, it was still the *Cape Argus* breaking the story.

In the age of flagging newspaper sales too, I had to be more than just an editor – I had to think about how to make the business of newspapers sustainable. How could we sell custom content to advertisers without sacrificing the integrity of the news pages? We experimented successfully with this model on the sports pages of the *Argus*, as corporates linked to a sporting code would pay to have their brands aligned to a column related to the sport. My reasoning was that sponsored sport content was less fraught with regard to ethical considerations than sponsoring news content. No one had any qualms about SuperSport having sports current affairs programmes or radio news bulletins being sponsored. Why should newspapers be different?

We invested in conversation points; the type of content people always think about but never get to read about in their newspaper. For example, why do so many coloured people in Cape Town have calendar months as their surnames? How do we get a community descended from slaves and the indigenous people of the Cape talking about their genealogy? We created a space for the homeless people of Cape Town to have a voice in the newspaper, which was powerful in that it gave power to the powerless and a voice to the voiceless. We allowed students involved in the #FeesMustFall movement to co-edit an edition of the *Cape Argus* because they felt the news media wasn't listening to their side of the story. They turned out to be far more astute about our challenges than we, the grown-ups, had given them credit for.

We listened actively. We listened to our readers, our newspaper sellers, the cleaner who vacuumed the worn and tired looking newsroom carpet right on deadline, the aunty who sold the oily samoosas in the canteen and the most junior of reporters. I tried to create as democratic a newsroom as a newspaper would allow. But ultimately, my (in)decision was final. The buck stopped with me. I carried the can. I was the hack with a grenade. Also, I only know of one instance in which a newspaper – involving the #FeesMustFall students – was successfully edited by committee, and to this day I still believe it was a fluke.

But most of all, we were staying true to the legacy of Darnell and Murray that the *Cape Argus* would be welcomed into the merchant's office and family home alike – a champion of good causes and non-partisan, but forthright. My only regret was that I wasn't able to see this journey through, as I was needed elsewhere in the business.

It was this period of my career that shaped the genesis of this book. It started by telling the then as yet untold story of a motorsport champion of colour who was never fully recognised for his achievements. The interview I did with motorsport veteran Armien Levy was an idea for a book that he had broached with me. But it started a weekly column of profiles I wrote in the *Cape Argus* about ordinary people from all walks of life doing extraordinary things. It was called the *Friday Files* and I would fly by the seat of my pants to produce this weekly 2 000-word feature to meet the tight deadlines.

That *Friday Files* column would be the first of more than 100 profiles over a two-year period, and my subsequent *Sunday Slice* column for the *Weekend Argus,* which – as the name suggests – was a little slice of life every week, helped to enhance my own skills as a storyteller. I would like to think it inspired those around me to become storytellers too. All the while, I dabbled with multimedia. I wasn't satisfied with a *Friday Files* interview unless it carried a video component too. The video was made available via a QR code in the *Cape Argus* – again a pioneer as the first newspaper in South Africa to experiment with enhanced content using augmented reality.

Some of the people I interviewed have since become dear friends who I am still in contact with. They are the real men and women who make South Africa work. I feel privileged that they allowed me to tell their stories and trusted me enough to know that I would do them justice. What you will read on the pages to follow are their stories. They are the back stories of what makes us tick as a nation and the narratives behind our psyche.

This book is dedicated to all the men and women who deserved to have their stories told, but who didn't have the kind of access they needed due to our unjust past, which existed in all spheres of life, including the media. Your determination is what drove me to tell your untold stories so that we could celebrate the uncelebrated.

South Africa is a complicated place. Some said we would never make it. We teetered on the brink of civil war, and many lives were lost in the months leading up to our first democratic election. To the world, we are a land of miracles that somehow finds a way to forge

HACK WITH A GRENADE

ahead. We find a way to laugh despite our many challenges, like unemployment, violent crime, and extreme poverty and inequality. We find a way when HIV/Aids ravages millions of our compatriots. We find a way in the face of wave upon wave of economic uncertainty. Still, we will find a way through this new challenge of COVID-19 too.

Yet, we take this resolve for granted. It is as if we forget our own strength in overcoming adversity. We sell ourselves short by believing the solutions to our problems lie elsewhere when the answers are within our reach. They are written in the stories we have passed on from generation to generation about the people of faith, the destitute, the redemption seeker, the restless youth, the forgotten heroes, the trailblazers, the suffering of the little children, the displaced, and the search for our true South African selves. This book tells the South African story through the eyes of its people.

In order to know where we are going, we need to know where we have been. As long as newspapers have stories to tell they will remain relevant. We have not even begun to scrape the surface of the many stories that remain untold and that can only make us richer for it. Those who are able to deliver those stories in the most innovative ways, regardless of the platforms, will lead the way.

Celebrated Nigerian author Chimamanda Ngozi Adichie reminded us of the power and the importance of storytelling during a Ted Talk in 2009. She said: 'Many stories matter. Stories have been used to dispossess and to malign. But stories can also be used to empower, and to humanise. Stories can break the dignity of a people. But stories can also repair that broken dignity.'

The newspaper as a medium can no longer afford to carry the first drafts of history. It needs to reimagine its role – as a storyteller of untold stories to entertain, to uplift, to educate, to advocate, to celebrate, to expose and to shine a light on injustice. Storytelling is a gift to humankind that we cannot live without. By re-accepting this role in society as story-tellers, newspapers can forge an unbreakable bond with audiences like never before. In order for that relationship to be authentic, newspapers and the media in general, need to go back to basics, and reclaim and jealously guard their position as purveyors of credible content.

It has been an immense honour and a privilege to be a hack with a grenade. It was the best fun I had while being paid. But the burden of responsibility was always with me. The knowledge that I was only as good as the last story I wrote, or the last edition of the paper I edited, kept me humble and hungry to be better tomorrow than I was yesterday. The knowledge that what I published could irrevocably shape someone's life kept me grounded.

If you are in the news business, may that burden of responsibility never fail you. We have a duty to ourselves and to each other to always do the right thing. Yes, we will make mistakes and that is certainly the case in media and newspapering; but how we respond to those mistakes counts. We have a responsibility to be fair, accurate, balanced and impartial, without fear or favour, and to provide comment that is premised on fact.

If you are a consumer of news, never forget the high price of your news, and support credible journalism. Journalists are often in the front lines where danger lurks so that society can be kept informed. Their storytelling allows us to make informed decisions. They risk life and limb, often in conflict areas or exposed to the elements or disease, to bring you the news. Think about that when next you pick up a publication, and think about the cover price. In life, you wouldn't trust anyone running around with a grenade. So, why would you trust just anyone to bring you the news?

(PS: No limbs were lost in the writing of this book – by grenades or otherwise).

30 July 2011. Archbishop Thabo Makgoba, Anglican Archbishop of Cape Town, leads a delegation from the Western Cape Religious Leaders' Forum (WCRLF) with Imam Rashid Omar, to a number of informal settlements in Khayelitsha to stand in solidarity with people without adequate sanitation. Photo: Jeffrey Abrahams. ©ANA Pictures

1 Remona finds Jesus in her toilet

There is nothing quite as fascinating and intriguing as faith. It moves people to be better versions of themselves – often with amusing consequences. Even more amusing is how the interpretation of organised religion makes people behave.

South Africans in particular have always had religion at the heart of all they do or try to justify. The architects of apartheid subverted the word of God to suit their evil ends. But in the seriousness of faith and religion in our beautiful country lies the source of great mirth too.

A few weeks before our daughter's second birthday, my wife was dissuaded from throwing a Peppa Pig-themed party for our little girl's classmates at school in a predominantly Muslim community because the parents would be upset. It's not like we'd have served pork – the eating of which is strictly forbidden for Muslims. We were thinking a few cupcakes and sweets on Peppa Pig-themed paper plates, serviettes and paper cups. But Peppa is a pig and 'We can't have that!' So, Disney princess-themed paper plates, serviettes and paper cups it was.

Perhaps my views on faith and religion are too liberal because I grew up in a Muslim household that was more open than most. I knew all the hymns we were taught at school and came home to a mother who encouraged me to sing them, because she knew them well too. Growing up, we were encouraged to have friends from all walks of life – no matter their background, race or religion. I was acutely aware that my household was different. My friends had very conservative views about mixing with those who were different – their parents frowned upon it.

I took an interest in religions, particularly Christianity, Islam and Judaism – the three dominant faiths here in the Western Cape. I was fascinated to learn that, even though we worshipped gods with different names and our customs were very different, there was more to keep us together than that which might hold us apart. And

I was always aware of a tension between the Muslim and Jewish communities locally because of the Middle East conflict. I could not grasp this tension, in light of my own experience of Jewish people that my family and I were in contact with, and those who I read about who had made a significant mark in the world. It just didn't tally. Later, I would of course realise that it was complicated. But that's a story for another day, and in my role as a newspaper editor I had to learn to leave my personal views at the door.

To this day, I teach my children what my parents taught me: tolerance, respect and understanding. My wife embraced Islam and so our young family celebrates Eid, Easter and Christmas. Our respective families attend each other's christenings, doepmals (which is the colloquial phrase for a christening in the Muslim community) and thikrs (which are Muslim prayer meetings). I made a point of taking my teenage son along to a bar mitzvah so that he can appreciate the coming-of-age, rite-of-passage for a Jewish boy his age.

But in the days leading up to Easter of 2005, my own relationship with religion and faith would be shaken – or shook, as the cool kids say these days. It all happened during my time at a newspaper that was as far removed from religion as you could imagine. Cape Town's newest tabloid, the *Daily Voice*, had launched just a few weeks prior. It was so racy that some well-known religious figures in the Cape were blaming its antics for ills of biblical proportions.

I'll never forget the night in March 2005. It was the week leading up to the Easter weekend. The news desk called to say a woman had 'spotted God in her backyard'. That was enough to pique my interest, and photographer Shawn Uys and I sped down the M5 highway to the scene of this story. It sounded hilarious. We couldn't wait to get there.

That night and that story was the moment I fell in love with tabloid journalism. It was way past the time our shift ended and yet we were both hungry for more. The *Daily Voice* was our newspaper and we were serving a new market of newspaper readers who always wanted to read about their home, the Cape Flats. Never before had a newspaper spoken to them the way the *Daily Voice* did. And no other newspaper covered the Cape Flats the way the *Daily Voice* was covering it. For Shawn, many of our colleagues and I, it was most satisfying, because we grew up on the Cape Flats, and understood the people and what they were going through. For too long they had been ignored by the newspapers that claimed to represent all the people of Cape Town. Now, for the first time ever, people were reading a newspaper that covered the things that were important to them. They felt an affiliation to the *Daily Voice*.

In those early days when the newspaper was launched, it dawned on me that our readers cared deeply for what they believed in, especially their faith and religion. Any story involving Jesus, Allah or Prophet Muhammad (Peace Be Upon Him) should be handled with care.

But there was no need for Shawn and I to be overly cautious when we arrived at the scene of this divine sighting. The stage was already set. More than a thousand people had filled the courtyard outside the Lavender Hill tenement block of council flats. They all wanted to witness the miracle inside. Shawn led the way, working his way through the crowd while flashing his press camera at people, as if it was a burning torch that could singe their flesh. Eventually, we made it to the front door of the house where the miracle had happened, but there was another huge obstacle in our way – a self-appointed security guard brandishing a whip that was known as an aapstert on the Cape Flats. This guy wasn't going to let anyone in. But some more deft non-verbal communication between Shawn (again brandishing his press camera) and the guard and we were soon inside the house.

We asked if we could see for ourselves what the woman had seen, and without much persuasion a young woman led us to a bathroom in the modest ground floor council flat. I was first and I walked carefully into the dark bathroom that had only a cistern and a bath hidden by a shower curtain. There was a small window where the only light, pale and white from the moon, was pouring into the loo.

'There, stand on the crate and see for yourself,' the girl said to me in Afrikaans. I then saw it and had to take a second look to believe what I was seeing. Right there was the image in the bathroom window.

'Oh. My. God. It's true,' I shouted at Shawn. 'You can see it. Like an angel with a sword on the glass.'

'Kak man,'[1] Shawn said, as he pushed me off the crate so he could take a look for himself. Without saying a word, he brought his Nikon with its wide-angle lens up to his nose and shot just one frame. A second later, he carefully studied the LCD screen on the back of his digital SLR camera and exclaimed, 'Perfect.'

And that was all Shawn was going to say about the miracle. Shawn had seen and done it all and had the pictures to prove it. He was about as tough as they came, but there was a look on his face that night that I hadn't seen before. The usual cynical grin was gone. At that moment neither of us could remember any of the jokes we cracked on the way to this story about the woman who had had a visit from the Lord just a few days before Easter. Instead, I was starting to think seriously about how I was going to reconcile my own beliefs as a Muslim with the miracle I had just witnessed.

I started to compose myself as Shawn and I made our way out of the bathroom with Remona Petersen, the young woman who had discovered the vision in the toilet window. Remona took us back to the living room where a pastor was now joining hands with members of the household and a church group that had arrived from afar. They were in the midst of an impassioned prayer.

'Thank you Lord for choosing this house and this community to bring us your message. There are people from as far as Worcester who have come to see Your miracle,' the pastor said.

I shot a knowing look at Shawn, but there was no need to because he was already shooting pictures of this amazing scene. I was in heaven – tabloid heaven. The people believed in the vision, and that was all the licence I needed to write a story that heavily referenced religion and get away with it. Heck, even I believed I had witnessed a miracle. Oh, did I mention this was just a few days before Easter?

The next move was to speak to Remona and gently persuade her during her interview that she shouldn't speak to any other newspaper. I had decided this story would put the *Daily Voice* on the map and would define what the newspaper was all about. Remona had the perfect script. She had been drinking in the living room when she spilled some of her beer on the living room floor. She had gone to fetch the mop and bucket in the bathroom. When she bent down, the light from the window had caught her eye. She claimed that was the moment she first saw the image of Christ in the window.

Remona had all the quotes to complement her story. 'I believe God has chosen me to send His message to the people of Lavender

Hill that they must stop living in sin and they must start working together,' she said.

While speaking to Remona, the family had decided – at the behest of the pastor – that they should allow the thousand-or-so people queued up outside to witness the miracle as well. That was when all hell broke loose. The crowd started pushing and now the self-appointed security guard had a reason to use his aapstert. Soon stones were being thrown at the flat. A window shattered. It was time to bail.

After order was restored, visitors went inside the house one after the other. After seeing the miracle for themselves they weren't disappointed. 'God is great,' said one woman. Another shouted: 'Praise the Lord, our Saviour.'

But a few young men standing on a staircase nearby were not convinced. One of them said: 'Hulle is mal. Daai lyk soos die Clover Danone mannetjie (They're mad. That looks like the little man in the Clover Danone yoghurt logo).'

I had to admit he was right. Now that he had pointed it out, I realised the image I had seen did look like the logo. But what did he know anyway? I was quite irritated at his attempt to diminish the miracle. After all, it wasn't every day one saw Jesus.

As we were heading to the car, someone tugged at my arm. It was another young woman, Nolene Vywers, with a pane of frosted glass in her hand – the same kind as the one in Remona's bathroom window. She told us: 'That's not Jesus. Come, let me show you.'

Nolene held up the glass to the light of the streetlamp and there it was. The same image I saw in Remona's window. But how could it be? Shawn shot a few frames and we were off. I wasn't going to let this latest revelation spoil an otherwise perfectly legitimate miracle. Besides, I had a kick-ass story to write about Jesus living in a family's toilet.

I explained the dilemma to our editor Karl Brophy – an Irishman who was a master of the tabloid form. He instinctively knew how we'd treat the story and the subsequent 'truth' about what we had seen. Karl had grown up on newsroom floors. His dad, Michael, was a distinguished editor. Karl had great instincts and understood the

Cape Flats. 'All poor communities are the same,' he would tell us. 'They have the same dreams, problems and aspirations.'

Karl, who wouldn't have been out of place in a newsroom on the once notorious UK-tabloid headquarters of Fleet Street, often pushed the envelope. The headline 'Jesus lives in my toilet', wouldn't have been my first choice, admittedly. (In fact, it made me grimace.) But Karl knew best, I thought. And most times he did. Karl's advice to me was to write the story the way Remona had experienced the miracle. 'The next day we'll explain to our readers what really happened,' he said.

Sound advice, I thought. Then I started to feel nervous about how the story would be received. But telling the yarn was a great deal of fun. I must have had a smile on my face while writing it, because Karl said to me: 'Let's see that smile when we run a story with the headline, "Muhammad lives in my samoosa!"'

It was a typical Karl comment.

The day after the big 'Jesus lives in my toilet' exclusive, I set about finding out the truth about the frosted windowpane. As it turned out, the type of frosted glass was called Spotlight. It had gone out of production some 20 years prior to Remona's miracle.

I managed to find a pane of Spotlight glass at a second-hand store in Main Road, Retreat. After some bargaining, the owner sold it to me for R100. Back at the office we put the glass to the test. And lo and behold, we found that the young woman who had trashed my miracle was right: this was no miracle. Any light cast behind the Spotlight design gave a similar angel-like reflection in the glass. So, the day after miracle, we ran the follow-up story as 'The Truth' – a classic tabloid ploy to explain what had really happened and allow the publication to milk a great story with a follow-up.

As I alluded to earlier, the *Daily Voice* skirted dangerously close to pissing a lot of people off with the way it covered religion and deities. In our first month of publication, a well-known evangelical pastor of a major church group blamed the *Daily Voice* for the lack of rain in the year it was launched. The pastor also blamed the *Daily Voice* for the plague that was on its way to Cape Town. What plague, you may ask. Ask the pastor.

It was quite understandable that there was a big backlash for the 'Jesus Lives in My Toilet' headline. We were getting hate mail and my fears seemed justified that Karl had gone too far this time.

Those days at the *Daily Voice* were an interesting personal journey for me with religion and how I fitted into this mix. I had my own little battles to fight. That first month after we launched, the local Muslim community radio station, the *Voice of the Cape*, kept hounding me for an interview. They wanted to know how I, as a Muslim, could write for a publication that had a topless woman on page 3.

I didn't even consider going on to the radio show because I would've been on a hiding to nothing. It would've been like stepping into the boxing ring with Mike Tyson in his prime (or at any stage of his career for that matter). They had already decided that the *Daily Voice* had little or no redeeming qualities. What could I possibly say to change their minds? Sure, a few nosy aunts were asking my parents some uncomfortable questions about my new job. But why did I have to defend holding down a job to the Muslim community? They didn't care about the great stories we were breaking on a daily basis. All the critics seemed to be doing was to comment on our brash headlines and our kamikaze picture editing that left little to the imagination.

Yet, slowly but surely, the so-called mainstream news outlets were nicking our exclusive stories and doing their own follow-ups. I wrote an investigative piece about how the former South African Rugby Union boss, Brian van Rooyen, was coining it with Cape Town's traffic speed cameras. I exposed how flawed the Labatt (Van Rooyen's company) traffic fine ticketing system was, but how Van Rooyen was still laughing all the way to the bank with the taxpayers' money. Soon every broadsheet paper in town had picked up on the story.

But the critics didn't care and seldom acknowledged our hard work. We were the rookies in town. As far as they were concerned, we were big mouths, mavericks and show-offs and they couldn't wait for us to fail. But we weren't doing anything different to what the mainstream media was doing. On the contrary, we had to be much more careful and ensure that our stories would stand up to scrutiny and the press code, as we were pushing the boundaries – hard. But it was all out there on the Cape Flats – an untapped market for stories that everyone else missed because they were too busy hunting with the pack. As Ray Joseph, my first news editor at the *Daily Voice*, put it: 'You can't make it up.'

It was one of these sensational investigative stories by my colleague and good friend, Elliott Sylvester, that led to an uncomfortable brush with the Muslim Judicial Council (MJC). Elliott and Shawn had uncovered an alleged Al Qaeda-like training camp operating in the Western Cape. But that wasn't all. The operatives of these terror training camps were allegedly recruiting kids from the Cape Flats.

Elliott didn't only have an interview with the mom of a 15-year-old boy recruited to the camp by a neighbour, but he had a picture as well – a photograph of a group of boys dressed in camouflage, and posing with replica assault rifles. The mom told Elliott of her concern after her son had been trained to handle a firearm and underwent a survival course during his school holidays. This was scary stuff.

A day after we published the story, *Daily Voice* publisher, Rashid Seria, and I (by then the news editor) were invited to the headquarters of the MJC. We were later told it was convenient to have both of us there because we were Muslim and we 'understand the issues'. But the only issue I knew about was that some assholes were training children in terrorism without their parents knowing and the *Daily Voice* had exposed it. End of story.

By the time I arrived at the MJC's HQ in Athlone I was already quite pissed off about the things they had said about Rashid and me. A paper published by a member of the MJC leadership said that both Rashid and I would suffer from the burning red coals that had been placed in our bellies and those of our families because we were working for the *Daily Voice*. I was ready for a fight.

Rashid was always the diplomat and the gentleman – a respected newspaper veteran and activist who had worked on Struggle publications like *South*. He had made it his mission to sell the *Daily Voice* to advertisers and the public, and was in a big way a kind of handbrake on Karl's wild antics.

Rashid went about explaining to the MJC's full executive – including the author of the hot coals paper – what the *Daily Voice* was all about. But it was like speaking to a brick wall. It was when we got to the crux of the matter that tempers began to fray: the terror training camp story. The MJC president started his deliberations by admitting that they knew about this training camp. But he said the next time we wrote such an explosive story about Muslims and terrorism in the Cape we should consult them. Why? So they could censor large parts of the story?

The MJC president went on to explain that a lot of mistakes were made when activity involving People Against Gangsterism and Drugs (Pagad) was at its height in the Western Cape. (This group had started in response to rife drug abuse and gangsterism.) Pagad was later branded an urban-terrorist organisation and was even banned by organisations like the FBI in the United States. The MJC didn't want those mistakes to be repeated. But the only mistake I – and the other reporters who covered the wave of urban terrorism in the late 1990s – saw was the MJC's lack of authority during the Pagad activity.

I left that meeting with a bad taste in my mouth and I was right to smell a rat, because the open-door policy the MJC executive promised never materialised. Their idea of consulting was telling us how and when we could use a picture of one of their leaders. A case in point was when the news desk received a complaint that we had carried a picture of the former MJC president on page 2. I looked at Rashid (by now we were the *Daily Voice's* liaisons with the Muslim community by proxy) and we both had bemused looks on our faces. Upon further inquiry, we were shocked to learn that when you closed the *Daily Voice*, the MJC president's face landed softly between the ample breasts of a Page 3 girl. The MJC believed we had done this deliberately and it was all they were talking about on *Voice of the Cape*. Sigh!

The MJC was on our backs again shortly after Jacob Zuma was elected president of the ANC in Polokwane in 2007. He visited them at their Athlone offices. They were, of course, asking for it when they endorsed Zuma – a man whose general set of values were, at best, questionable. The *Daily Voice* ran a front-page headline that screamed, 'Mshini Wam Salaam', with an accompanying photoshopped picture of Zuma wearing a fez. It was hilarious and went down well with our readers. It stirred a massive debate among Muslims as well, who couldn't believe the MJC had given Zuma the thumbs up. The MJC President called to say that the *Daily Voice* had it all wrong with this story, but couldn't explain how we had got it wrong.

But it was not only the MJC that tried to prescribe to us. Even Pagad tried to negotiate us into dropping the Page 3 girl for just one day. The organisation went as far as banning the *Daily Voice* from press conferences because of the topless girl on page 3.

At the time, the Page 3 device was the differentiator for the *Daily Voice* in a bid by management not to ruin sales of the *Cape Argus*. Later, management would dump the Page 3 girl in favour of attracting retail ads; but at that time it was a non-negotiable.

Pagad had realised the importance of the tabloid's reach on the Cape Flats. Prominent members of the organisation had offered the newspaper an exclusive interview with their leader Abdus-Salaam Ebrahim, who was freed from prison in September 2008, but on condition that the paper drop the Page 3 girl on the day the interview was published. But Elliott – by now editor of the *Daily Voice* – told them to piss off.

And of course, the pastor who had warned of the plague was also never too far behind in trying to shut the *Daily Voice* down. His latest campaign against the paper happened during the reign of terror of a serial murderer on the Cape Flats, called the 'Jesus Killer'. He was given this nickname by the community of farmworkers he terrorised because he had the word Jesus tattooed on his face. For once, the *Daily Voice* wasn't responsible for the nickname.

It didn't matter to the pastor that respectable papers like *Die Burger* also called the wanted man the Jesus Killer. Fortunately, the killer was eventually caught. But I couldn't help thinking that the pastor could have put his energy to better use by condemning the evil of this crazed serial killer and telling people why this should never happen again, rather than calling for a mass boycott of the *Daily Voice*.

Religion can be a very beautiful and important part of life, but it becomes distorted by people. I made peace with being a Muslim and working at the *Daily Voice*. I never claimed to be a saint, and I was proud to be associated with a newspaper that would not be bullied by people who carried the heavy tag of religious authority.

Tabloids around the world don't suffer fools gladly. The *Daily Voice* and its rival, *Die Son*, were something of a novelty when they launched. They used the Cape Flats dialect in their stories, prided themselves in producing well-designed newspapers, and actually had a sense of humour. They fitted into the Cape Flats culture like koesisters[2] on a Sunday morning, the minstrels on Tweede Nuwejaar[3] and walking around in the street with rollers in your hair.

But behind the slick design and beyond the irreverence were real, well-written and well-researched exposés that stood up to the strictest media laws. We had to be so much more careful than the broadsheets because we were taking many more risks and pushing the envelope. By 2009, the tabloids had grown significantly in readership – no mean feat when newspaper sales were flagging everywhere else.

It was in this vein that I approached my time from 2009 to 2015 as editor of both the *Cape Argus* and *Cape Times* (two of Cape Town's most influential, leading daily newspapers), i.e. I aimed for the same high standard and investigative rigour. It is important for the media at large to not only reflect the news of the day, but to also enrich the debate with different and also dissident and diverse opinion. We are guided by the South African Press Code, which advocates freedom of speech and freedom of expression that is tempered with responsibilities that include limiting harm and providing comment, opinion and analysis that is accurate, unbiased, fair and balanced. It also binds us to steer away from giving a platform to hate speech, discrimination, bigotry and prejudice, and instead to place a premium on values like tolerance of religious and ideological beliefs.

In our day-to-day work as journalists we are often forced to make decisions on what is relevant, newsworthy and in the public interest. It is the telling of the South African story – warts and all. It's a celebration of all that is right and good, but also a fearless critique of our failings, with a relentless role of holding those in power – in government and the private sector – to account.

It is in this space that the interfaith community in our country – members of various religious groups who work towards common good – plays a crucial role as a moral barometer and a guardian of values and social justice. Where does the media fit into this? It is a conduit to reflecting this important voice in our democracy. But the only way the media can do this is if those involved in interfaith movements remain relevant, and address the issues that affect our democracy.

Patience is considered a virtue in most religions. And so the South African faith communities were extremely patient with our fledgling democracy in its early days, taking care not to rush into chastising this young child who had a lot of growing up to do. But in August 2012, there was a shift in temperature. Anglican Archbishop of Cape Town, Thabo Makgoba, established an anti-corruption movement within the Western Cape Religious Leaders Forum, and called on the major religions to participate in the movement. The religious leaders issued a stern warning to political leaders about their reluctance to deal with corruption. They said that the silence of political leaders and the public would lead to society's crumbling, and warned that the pursuit of money and power was threatening our young democracy.

At the launch in Khayelitsha, Makgoba said: 'We as religious leaders are still learning to speak truth to power, but are afraid to speak truth to our friends who are in power.' At the same event, Catholic Archbishop Stephen Brislin said that, in recent times, corruption had broken the trust between members of the public and their leaders. Chief Rabbi Warren Goldstein said that the moral regeneration of society required that children should learn about the 'bill of responsibility' at schools – that with every right came a responsibility.

And so, a multi-faith anti-corruption movement was born, with leaders of different faiths speaking as one voice. A declaration calling for an end to corruption was signed by 18 religious leaders and 44 other signatories in Cape Town. For very good reasons, this powerful statement dominated front pages and news bulletins.

But this was not a new or foreign trend in this country. When South Africa was at its lowest point, at the height of the Struggle against apartheid, it was the faith leaders who were an important voice against injustice. Ordinary men and women put their ideological and theological differences aside for the greater good. Some of the biggest heroes of our Struggle were Muslims, Christians and Jews who fought alongside each other for a free South Africa – just think of Ahmed Kathrada and Denis Goldberg, for example, and heroes of the cloth like Archbishop Desmond Tutu, Father Trevor Huddleston and Imam Abdullah Haron.

I believe it is the responsibility of organised religion to continue leading the charge and leading our Struggle. But this is a different struggle. It is a struggle against poverty, unemployment, corruption, indifference, bigotry, injustice, discrimination, gender violence, women and child abuse, and the apathy many display towards active citizenry. We need the voices of our faith leaders to be the voices of reason – and the critical voices when children are raped and murdered, when another child victim is claimed in gang crossfire, when drug abuse becomes so rife that a mother is moved to kill her own son, when mineworkers are gunned down at the hands of our police force, when our road death toll is in danger of breaking new records, when protesters adopt unsavoury and unhygienic ways to voice their dissent, when graft and corruption becomes endemic in public and private life, and when we are in danger of being on the road to becoming a failed state.

I believe Cape Town's interfaith movement is the most vibrant in South Africa and, arguably, in the world. Very few global cities have the kind of interfaith solidarity and co-existence that we have in Cape Town. It is something that needs to be cherished and celebrated and the media has an important role to play in doing so.

As editor of the *Cape Argus*, in particular, I published a series of prominent opinion articles in 2012, penned by interfaith leaders about their fight against corruption. None of the opinion pieces were preachy; they honed in directly on the bread-and-butter issues of the day. In these pieces, clerics like Rashied Omar, Mickey Glass and Makgoba spread the universal message that corruption would no longer be tolerated.

In an article written in 2010 by Imam Rashied Omar, Imam of the Claremont Main Road mosque and former chair of the Western Cape Religious Leaders Forum, he very astutely summed up the potential and gravitas of the interfaith community. Omar has consistently spread the message that we have strength in our diversity. 'Interreligious dialogue and solidarity has been one of the major beneficiaries of the post-apartheid dispensation,' he wrote. 'The new non-racial and democratic government under the moral leadership of first president Nelson Mandela has worked hard to sustain and further develop the legacy of interreligious solidarity forged in the Struggle against apartheid.

'In response to a call by Mandela, religious leaders have set up an interreligious Forum of Religious Leaders to liaise between government and religious communities. Ironically, however, the post-apartheid South African state's overt policy of religious pluralism and interreligious harmony has not been sufficiently buttressed by religious leaders at the civil-society level, and consequently it has not sufficiently filtered down to the grassroots. This is an anomaly that interreligious activists in South Africa are aware of, and are working hard to correct.'

The bit that resonated most with me was when Omar wrote: 'For me, the litmus test of "good" and "bad" religion is the extent to which we are willing to embrace the "other", whoever that other may be. We need to recognise our common humanity and see others as a reflection of ourselves. If we do not try to "know" the other, how can we ever "know" the Divine?'

What role does the media play in promoting interfaith harmony? A central one. Like the messengers of gospels of the Divine word, journalists are modern-day messengers with an obligation to truth and justice.

For the millions of people who live on the Cape Flats, that interfaith is a daily reality. Muslims visit their Christian neighbours' homes on Christmas Day and the favour is returned on Eid day. Many Cape Flats homes, like my household, will happily put up a Christmas tree and, a few months later, observe all the tenets of the holy Muslim month of Ramadan. When I was growing up in Mitchells Plain, and later Woodstock, the athaan – the Muslim call to prayer – was a signal to kids of all faiths that it was time to go inside, time to go to mosque, time for homework or the bath before bedtime. That tradition was born in the streets of District Six decades earlier, before people were forcibly removed and settled on the Cape Flats. Whether they were Muslim or Christian or Jewish, they would attend a church service, visit a synagogue or pray at a mosque with their friends.

It was no surprise at all that people from all faiths came out in their thousands to support the athaan delivered by Muir Street Mosque in District Six in Ramadan in 2019. The mosque, which was celebrating its 100th year, received a single complaint from a resident who had recently moved into the area. The City of Cape Town was obliged to investigate the complaint as a noise disturbance. But due to intense pressure from members of the public, the City's ruling party was forced to consider a review of its bylaw governing noise disturbances to exclude acts of worship, like the call to prayer or church bells. This was interfaith and religious plurality in action. Our respect and deep sense of common humanity makes us fiercely protective of our diversity – religious and otherwise.

But it was the events of that night leading up to Easter 2005, when Remona saw the image of Christ in the bathroom window, that made me look at miracles in a very different light – no pun intended. There have been others during my time at the *Daily Voice* that colleagues have covered. Like the time when a house in Atlantis was burnt down and the only thing that remained was a painting of Jesus and the couch above which it hung. There were also the two butchers from different parts of the Cape Flats who swore they found the name of Allah written in Arabic in sinew in cuts of meat. But none were quite as definitive (or not, as it would later turn out) as the image of Jesus that Remona believed she had seen in her toilet window.

Who are you and I to decide what is a miracle anyway? The big lesson I learnt from the experience was that if people believe in something then that is sometimes more powerful than what science can prove or disprove. Remona, her family and an entire community saw Jesus in the window of a toilet and it turned them into believers. It made her want to change her life. Isn't that the miracle?

10 October 2017. Danny Oosthuizen at the Expresso Studios in Sea Point, Cape Town, after he participated in a TV segment on the breakfast show on the occasion of World Homeless Day. Photo: Unknown. ©*ANA Pictures*

2 *Danny and the invisible people*

We sat with heavily furrowed brows in the corridor of the Cape Town Magistrate's Court, wondering what to do next. Courts are terrible places. They can be great levelers too – even when you have the best resources available to get you out of a spot of bother. But those odds increase the less you have.

We sat on two hard wooden benches outside the courtroom: me (a whole regional executive editor of a leading newspaper group), *Cape Argus* Assistant Editor Lance Witten and Pat Eddy and Mark Williams of the Central City Improvement District (CCID). I also had legal advice at the ready, thanks to a top lawyer friend, Madhni Arnold.

On this Monday morning in January 2018, there was little hope we were going to get bail for Danny Oosthuizen. It wasn't because Danny was accused of murder, armed robbery, rape or any other such heinous crime. In the bigger scheme of things, his offence was serious, but not serious enough to deny him bail. But the reason we were worried Danny would be denied bail was due to a simple fact that wasn't at all Danny's fault. Danny was homeless.

Why all this effort then for a homeless guy, you may be asking?

Allow me to introduce Danny properly though. He isn't a criminal. He is also more than the sum of the circumstances that dictated his life. Our journey with Danny began two years earlier, when I was the *Cape Argus* editor. I had been invited by reformed 28s prison gang leader, Magadien Wentzel, to meet a few homeless people he had chosen to work with in his new role as a peace ambassador. Magadien's own story is fascinating and he is an incredible example of resilience. But more about Magadien later.

Magadien had asked me to come to the Service Dining Rooms in Roeland Street in the Cape Town CBD one afternoon. Here, homeless people are assisted with a hot meal, and temporary work when it is available. Magadien had wanted me to speak about my job as the editor of the *Cape Argus*. But I was so surprised by what I found at the Service Dining Rooms that I soon became engrossed in the stories of the homeless people there. The visit became less about my job and more about these people, who had dreams and aspirations like you and me. They had families and one of them was expecting a baby. There was a university graduate and a man who battled to articulate how a series of unfortunate events landed him in jail.

I suspected, too, that Magadien was keen to show me just how far his own development had come. He was in charge here, having started a food garden across the road from the Service Dining Rooms. Magadien put his new friends to work growing fresh produce that would eventually be sold to members of the public and restaurants in the CBD. From the smile on his face, I could see his contentment and self-satisfaction – a new sense of purpose for a tormented soul.

I left the Service Dining Rooms and remember walking back to the office in Newspaper House with a head spinning full of ideas. We would tell the stories of the homeless people of Cape Town. No, scratch that. We would allow the homeless to tell their own stories. Give a voice to voiceless. By now, I was so excited I was almost running back to the newsroom.

First chance I got that afternoon at the news conference I broke the news to my team. We would do an editorial series on the homeless people of Cape Town. My idea was met with silence. I could feel the eye-rolling. These guys worked in a daily newsroom covering murder, mayhem and menace every day. They had seen it all. How would we make stories about homeless people news? No one cared about homeless people, surely?

But this was just the thing. The *Cape Argus* was in trouble and it wasn't alone. Newspapers were in trouble. And unless we found a novel way of re-introducing our job of being storytellers, we would have to face the fact that sooner or later newspapers were going to die. I had experimented during this second bite at editing the paper with moving the *Cape Argus* away from being a newspaper of record. People don't come to newspapers for news, was my rationale. They wanted depth, analysis and understanding. They wanted to be entertained. They could get their news from the radio or on Twitter. We needed to give them something more meaningful for them to buy the paper.

My reasoning worked, because I managed to persuade one of the best storytellers I have ever worked with to head up the series on homeless people. Lance Witten had worked in TV, radio and then newspapers. He was skilled in multimedia storytelling. This was the guy for the job.

After Lance and photographer Henk Kruger started meeting homeless people and photographing them, it was difficult to get them back to the office. They couldn't get enough of the stories and the richness of the lives of the people they met. Henk in particular – a man of few words –was moved by the incredible sadness etched into the faces of these lives we seldom acknowledge.

Two weeks or so later, I had had enough of begging Lance to show me the first drafts of what he had gathered on the streets. It was time for Lance to come back to the office to write this series. It was time for Henk to show me what images he had. I had given Lance and Henk a simple brief: I wanted authentic stories of homeless people telling their stories in their own voices. I didn't want pictures of homeless people sleeping rough or scratching in rubbish bins or begging for food at traffic lights. I wanted Henk, especially, to capture images of the homeless people we were profiling at their most dignified – in the way that we would photograph the mayor or the president for a profile interview.

Once Lance had his list of stories for the series and Henk had put together his images, I called a special news conference. We had about 14 or so pieces on individuals who had incredible stories to tell. I repeated the brief I had given to Lance and Henk to the production team (which included Assistant Editor Robyn Leary, Chief Sub Colin Appolis and News Editor Jade Otto), that I wanted to portray the stories of the homeless people in the most dignified way possible. And that is how the name 'The Dignity Project' was born.

Our talented graphic designer, Rowan Abrahams, started playing with designs for a logo. Understandably, he came up with very clever designs featuring corrugated cardboard – symbolism of some of the material the homeless people used on the street. If the point of the project was to extend the dignity of the homeless people who were participating, we felt that the look and feel of the project should not evoke those elements that showed them at their worse. We settled on a simple, yet elegant font and design. In the back of my mind though, I knew that while we had a good editorial series that would get the people of this city talking, it lacked that big thing. It needed something special to help us land The Dignity Project with the people of a city that had become desensitised to homeless people. I needed to shake the Cape.

Then I remembered that Lance had mentioned in passing that he had met a particular homeless man while gathering his interviews – a homeless man who could write. The guy had offered to write a column for the paper. I hadn't given it much thought until then. So I asked Lance if we could get this guy to send us some of his writing so that I could take a look. It took another day or two, but when the piece arrived, I immediately knew that I had found the big drawcard to put The Dignity Project front and centre in the hearts and minds of Capetonians.

Danny Oosthuizen could write. Sure, the writing needed a bit of polishing, but this guy could tell a story, had a great turn of phrase and an excellent sense of humour to boot. I wanted to meet Danny and propose something that would disrupt his life and the lives of the folks who worked at the *Cape Argus* in a big way, in a good way and in a potentially life-changing way.

It was a Sunday morning in April 2016 when Lance brought Danny into the newsroom for the first time. We were to launch The Dignity Project the next day and that *Cape Argus* of that Monday was to be historic. For the first time ever, in the history of newspapers, in what the tabloids would call a 'World Exclusive', a homeless person would write the front page lead article of a mainstream newspaper. What is more, we would be launching a daily column that would run for the duration of The Dignity Project. When the three-week series concluded, Danny's Diary – the name of the new column – would run every Tuesday in the *Cape Argus*. And Danny would be paid for his efforts.

When I met Danny, he didn't know about my grand plan. I was very conscious of making a good first impression, because I needed Danny, then 47 years old, to buy into the plan. I ended up saying something ridiculous to him about how I imagined him being taller!

Perhaps my awkward moment was down to my eagerness to show Danny he was like everyone else in the *Cape Argus* newsroom.

It was an overwhelming experience for Danny too. He remembered the day clearly in a subsequent profile piece I did on him for my weekly *Cape Argus* Friday Files column: 'When you walk into a place like this, you know, this building is very intimidating. You see a big staircase and marble and a portrait of Madiba on the wall. I thought, "Oh my, you don't look like these people, you don't smell like these people."

'Then I meet the editor, who tells me he thought I was taller. I ran to the church across the road. I sat there and thought: what am I going to do now? I came back and I felt uncomfortable, because I was intimidated by these people who had years of experience and are qualified and have written stories that have made major headlines. Here I come from the streets and write my diaries and tell the world who is who in the zoo.

'But they actually embraced me. The fact that my stuff wasn't really changed made me even more paranoid. On the Monday morning that my picture was on the front page, the security guard here looked at me and said, "You're in trouble. Your face is in the newspaper."'

The *Cape Argus* edition of 11 April 2016 was the talk of the town. The Dignity Project was featured on radio stations and was all the rage on social media. The *Cape Argus* was lauded, and I knew we were on to something great. There, splashed on the front page, was the headline: 'I'm just like you but I'm homeless.' Danny's lead story, written in the first-person narrative, was accompanied by Henk's beautiful portrait of him standing in the centre of Cape Town's railway station platform building as the hustle and bustle of commuters passed him by.

And boy, did Danny rise to the occasion. In the intro of his article and the opening paragraphs, Danny opened his heart to the people of Cape Town: 'My name is Danny Oosthuizen. I am one of many homeless people in Cape Town.

'When people look at us, they don't see the strength that we have. We are resilient. We're tough. But that doesn't mean we don't need love.

'Yes, it's true. Some of us are spiritually and psychologically damaged. Wouldn't you be? There is a constant struggle for recognition in society.

'And maybe sometimes we even feel like we don't belong in society. I mean, we don't look the part, we don't smell the part, but we're human too.

'People often look at us and think all we want are material things. I'm not saying we don't need things – everyone needs things. But we don't want your money and material things; we need engagement, we want to be part of society.'

Danny ended the article with this powerful message: 'What do I want you to do about it? Oh, please, I don't want your pity. I don't need you to feel sorry for me.

I want you to talk to me.

I want you to see me.

I want you to acknowledge my humanity.

I want you to greet me.

I'm human too.

Sincerely,

Danny'

In his column on the inside pages, Danny brought to life for readers what life was like for the homeless people of Cape Town. He was funny and engaging, and it helped a great deal that he could literally write the living crap out of his lived experience. His stories were also a stark reminder that any one of us can easily end up on the streets.

His first inside-page column, which accompanied his front-page lead, started like this: 'Not so long ago I lived in Green Point (The Rockwell) and earned good money. I was wearing labels and ate out at some of the best restaurants in town. I had a very comfy life. Then life took a turn...

'When living on the streets is your only option, it comes as a shock. You are exposed to things you would never have dreamt of. But I had the time to learn so much about myself and how strong I am.

'You also learn how society can choose to turn a blind eye and how some people go out of their way to help.

'Living on the streets can be harsh at times. Not to mention dangerous. But, in general, we do the best we can with what we have. Honestly, I started using tik (meth).[4] It kept me awake at night. Also, I could go for days without a meal as it suppresses your appetite. I went from a size 32 to a size 28 in four days. It was not a solution to the problem, so I stopped.'

Danny would later explain in subsequent columns how he filed his pieces for the *Cape Argus*. He went to the library and used the 30 minutes of free Wi-Fi available to him, making sure to email his unfinished draft to himself so that he could complete it at a different city library.

But I had an ulterior motive too. I insisted that Danny work in our newsroom, side-by-side with the *Argus* journos and production staff and sit in on our news conferences. He was well-read and made telling contributions to those conferences, giving his unique perspective on the global events that shape our lives.

He needed a space to work and couldn't trek from library to library. But my real reasoning was simple: how could we present a sincere collection of stories about the homeless when we had our own deep-seated prejudices? We needed to experience Danny's daily reality – that he was HIV positive, gay and homeless too, and how a minor thing like taking a shower was a major thing in his world.

There were a few awkward teething problems with sharing the workspace with a homeless individual. My colleagues started asking me if they could bring toiletries and clothing for Danny. My response was that Danny could speak very well for himself, so they should ask him. There were also a few complaints that Danny was using the newsroom shower (yes, the newsroom had a shower because a previous editor was a cyclist and had had one installed). My response was that Danny could keep using the showers, and if anyone had a problem with that, they would answer to me.

It was a slow process, but Danny eventually became immensely popular amongst the readers. He endeared himself to them and wrote about everything, including his most personal moments and thoughts. One column in particular that moved Capetonians, was when Danny wrote about how difficult it was for a homeless woman on the streets during her menstrual cycle. But the growing popularity had other unforeseen consequences, as all the attention was sometimes over-whelming for him. And each time Lance and I had to talk Danny down from 'the ledge' because it was overwhelming at times. There was the time a security guard popped into the office and gave him the most beautiful toiletry bag filled with all he needed to keep himself well-groomed. Then a woman emailed him to ask if he could meet her at a specified address. We were all super curious. At the meeting, the woman presented him with a set of double tickets to the Mariah Carey concert at the Cape Town Stadium!

Danny was soon featured on radio stations and morning television shows, talking about the plight of homeless people, and sharing his experiences with an even wider audience. He attracted corporate attention and the folks from GrandWest casino invited him to attend their version of a CEO Sleepover, with further plans for Danny to address their staff as a motivational speaker. Another corporate gave him and a plus-one one-night complimentary stay at the 5-star Table Bay Hotel at the V & A Waterfront, where celebrities like Madonna, Michael Jackson and a slew of presidents had stayed.

A few weeks after Danny was settled in the newsroom, I found him glued to the computer screen with a set of headphones on his head. On his screen was an online writing and journalism course. Danny was busy educating himself. It was a profound moment for me. I didn't say anything, but thought that, as the 'homed', we have so many resources, but there are so many things we take for granted. Here was a guy grabbing every opportunity to improve his circumstances.

All the while, the hardened attitudes towards homeless people in Cape Town were softening. Danny reported that even the authorities – law enforcement officers from the City of Cape Town and members of the South African Police Services – were a lot more sympathetic. Before The Dignity Project there was a hate-hate relationship between homeless people and the cops. But the authorities' usual iron-fist approach was starting to thaw. The Central City Improvement District, in particular, led the way in helping to change attitudes. They had a tricky task to keep the business people they represented happy, while trying to ease relations between the homeless and the public.

Apart from Danny's advocacy, The Dignity Project, as an editorial series, showcased a number of other homeless heroes. Among them was Magadien, who lent his invaluable expertise and lived experience to his new homeless friends. Jesse Laitinen, who headed up the non-profit organisation, StreetScapes, threw her full weight behind the *Cape Argus* and a collaboration soon saw homeless people selling gourmet sandwiches to office workers with the yummy ingredients supplied courtesy of Magadien's veggie garden. The Doppio Zero eatery, located next to the *Cape Argus* headquarters in St George's Mall, started stocking fresh produce from the garden too. Lance had managed to broker workspace for a homeless man who made the most amazing marimba drums. Then there was the remarkable story of JP Persent – a homeless man himself whose personal circumstances improved just marginally enough for him to open a soup kitchen for other homeless people.

There was a fair share of villains too. The *Cape Argus* heard several accounts from homeless people about the kind of corruption and thievery engaged in by the managers of shelters. It was pretty much the same narrative, that big retailers would send loads of perishable goods to shelters that were nearing the expiry date. But the managers would cherry pick the best of the donations for themselves and the homeless people, who the food was destined for, would get the scraps.

Then there were the stories about shelters that were charging homeless people for beds, even though they were already being paid for the beds by the Social Development Department at the City of Cape Town. The Mayoral Committee Member at the time appeared indifferent and quite defensive about the claims made about the shelters. Danny would often lock horns with this Mayoral Committee Member in letters and in his column. But he remained dignified in his responses, even though there was reason for him to be furious. Two years later, this defensiveness and indifference would set the tone for some draconian moves by the City of Cape Town.

I remember how defeated I felt after reading headlines in July 2019 that the City of Cape Town had started fining homeless people for sleeping rough. There was an outcry from civil society, which slammed the municipality for being inhumane. Weeks later, I couldn't believe Mayor of Cape Town Dan Plato's stance on the matter. By then the city had issued a total of 199 fines to homeless people. He was quoted in the *Cape Argus* as saying at a full council sitting: 'There is no by-law just for homeless people, that is absolute nonsense. By-laws are for all of society. We cannot dare to start making exceptions. There is no reason to sleep on the street or to set up illegal structures on sidewalks. There are beds in shelters: they are not full. But some of those who should be making use of the shelters flat out refuse the services available.'

In a speech that could easily have been attributed to Boris Johnson or Donald Trump, Plato added: 'We have pioneered Safe Spaces in this city, we heavily subsidised the many shelters that still have empty beds, we have job creation opportunities for our homeless, skills development programmes, computer training programmes and much more. But we cannot force those who don't want to make use of these programmes to get help. It is up to them to want to make use of the services we provide.'

Perhaps Plato should have started where the *Cape Argus* dared to tread back in 2016 – by engaging homeless people. He would have learnt first-hand how these shelters and his own council had relegated the homeless to second-class citizens and were criminalising homelessness and poverty. As far back as 2010, the City of Cape Town had made the cynical move of dumping the homeless people of the Cape Town CBD at the far reaches of Blikkiesdorp – a temporary relocation area with wooden structures where the marginalised of the city usually end up – in a bid to 'clean up' the city ahead of the FIFA World Cup that the Mother City would host later that year.

But it is this broader criminalisation of poverty and homelessness that had a knock-on effect on everything else. Pollsmoor Prison, where most homeless people who commit a crime end up, is overrun. It is a factory for the recruitment of prison gangsters. It is a university of crime that is hard to escape. By issuing a fine that has little to no chance of being paid, the inevitable conclusion will be a stint in prison at Pollsmoor, awaiting trial. The courts have no time for those who can't verify a fixed home address. It's 'go to jail, move directly to jail, do not pass "Begin", do not collect R20 000'.

This brings me back to that Monday in January 2018 when Danny was appearing in court. There we were, wondering how we were going to get our friend out of jail. He was already in Pollsmoor, awaiting trial. A homeless man with no fixed abode. A man who was gay and HIV-positive. Leaving Danny in Pollsmoor would've been as good as giving him a death sentence.

At the same time, Danny was in the wrong, and he knew it. He had relapsed and had been arrested for drug possession. He could barely look at us because he felt so ashamed. Later he would write in his column that he was fearful that everything that he had worked so hard to build up, like his job at the *Cape Argus*, would be taken away from him by this one mistake.

In his typical way, Danny bared his soul to the *Cape Argus* reader. He wrote: 'I messed up and I am deeply sorry. I have given people sleepless nights and I let myself down.'

And Danny had a real knack for speaking directly to the readers.

'Dear reader, I found myself on the other side of the law a couple of weeks ago. For nine days I found myself in a place I would not even wish my worst enemy to be in. I will spare you the details. I am sure there are people out there who can relate.

'Since November last year, I cut myself off from everybody. I hate conflict. And I cannot really pinpoint the reason I felt like this. The festive season is a time for celebration. For me, it was sheer torture. It meant loneliness.

'Everybody I knew was busy with their families, which is quite the normal thing to do. I can't explain this, but I felt left behind. And instead of being honest about how I felt I walked away. The worst thing that can happen to me is to be left on my own. Demolition, baby.

'All my life I had this spot of darkness in my soul. I thought everybody had it. But I realised recently I created this space myself. And it is filled with broken dreams, resentment, self-hate and despair. There are boxes and they have labels on them. Orphan, Gay, HIV-positive, Department of Insecurity, Ministry of Self-doubt, to mention a few. The air in here is heavy. No windows. The soul is starved.

'Here one feeds on suicidal thoughts and self-destructive ideas. "I am not good enough" is the name of the main road. A dodgy cul-de-sac. I am my biggest enemy, saboteur. But ultimately I am the one who will break these chains of bondage.

'Out of this hellish experience came something money could never buy: unconditional support, love and care. From where I never thought it would. My mind felt like a microwave by the time I got into the courtroom. I could not see a positive outcome for myself.

'The very people I despised not so long ago, the very people I regarded as public enemy number one were there. As I enter the court, all cuffed up, I walk into Mrs Pat Eddy. Then Mr Mark

Williams, both from the Central City Improvement District. Still unsure why they were there.

'They were there to fight for me. Mark got me a place to stay. I was overwhelmed by their support. I then see Mr Gasant Abarder from Independent Media. "Oh shit, I am fired!" I said to myself. Stupid me. But Gasant was there to confirm I'm still working for the *Cape Argus*. There was a letter to this effect from the *Cape Argus* editor.

'I also got a letter from (Jesse Laitinen) to say they have a diversion plan ready for me. I was a first offender. The magistrate made it very clear that I will be monitored. Free to go. I say this with humility – I have people who dearly care for me. I had taken it for granted. Gasant said something profound: "I cannot judge you. I don't know what it is like to be Danny."

'Now I need to love myself and find redemption.'

Jesse Laitinen of StreetScapes had supplied Lance with a letter for the court, giving a commitment that Danny would be included in a diversion programme for drug abusers. Pat Eddy and Mark Williams of the Central City Improvement District (CCID), who had befriended Danny over the past years, were genuinely concerned, and Mark was ready to give the court an assurance that he would personally take Danny to the shelter once he was released.

Aziz Hartley, the current editor of the *Cape Argus*, was on standby to pay the bail money. And my lawyer friend, Madhni Arnold, managed his diary skillfully that day to make sure he could appear pro-bono for Danny.

Earlier my heart had sunk when the prosecutor in the same court that Danny was to appear in told the court during argument for a postponement in another matter that the average turnaround time for a case was about six months. That was if you were lucky.

Were it not for the efforts of this small, but extraordinary, group of people, Danny might have found himself at Pollsmoor for six months. This group was neither going to judge Danny nor condone what he did. But what we couldn't allow, if we could help it at all, was for him to spend six months in Pollsmoor.

I was so grateful for Pat and Mark. Mark had originally informed me about Danny's arrest. Pat and Mark walked a fine line as part of the social development side of the CCID, an organisation that also has an obligation to businesses. It is a complicated process. It has to balance heart and mind by looking after the welfare of our city centre's most vulnerable, while at the same time shielding businesses against the inevitable misdemeanours that come with homelessness. The two worlds collide often.

Danny was released on a warning, due largely to the efforts of these selfless individuals. But Danny also put in the hard yards. He fostered a working relationship with the CCID, where there was once deep suspicion and animosity. He helped soften attitudes between the CCID and the homeless, and between the homeless and the homed.

Lessons were learnt and Danny was, of course, as remorseful as ever. But Danny was worth the effort. We owed him. He had taught us much about our common humanity and how to respect those who have nothing. Lance and I encouraged Danny to start writing his memoirs and he suggested the title – 'Memoirs of a Life Almost Wasted'. We joked about giving Danny the new nickname of 'Shawshank' – inspired by the film 'The Shawshank Redemption'.

Danny saved himself that day – and his investment paid off. But what of the 199 homeless people who have become criminalised because they can't pay their fines? Fines that were issued simply because they had nowhere else to stay. As we heard time after time during The Dignity Project and in Danny's columns, those who didn't want to stay in a shelter had good reason not to.

I will forever be grateful for having met Danny and for the lessons he taught me. It takes more to walk the miles of Danny's shoes than we care to imagine. I keep reminding myself that I am one pay cheque away from being homeless. It is a humbling thought. I am grateful to Danny that I am able to see and respect the people who were once invisible to me and how his work has made us all better people.

* At the time this chapter was written, Danny had just celebrated his 50th birthday, and had been diagnosed with terminal stage cancer. He was given a few months to live. In his dying days, he set about completing a bucket list of things he wanted to achieve before he died. He passed away in hospital, 30 minutes before midnight, on 5 January 2020.

20 July 2015. Magadien Wentzel is a former member of the 28s prison gang and the subject of the book, *The Number*. He wants redemption and for society to give him a second chance after changing his life. Photo: David Ritchie. ©*ANA Pictures*

3 Magadien Wentzel's quest for redemption

'Magadien Wentzel is here to see you. He's there in the smoking room,' said my newsroom colleague. What? They let him in? Oh no, this guy was here to kill me!

Fourteen years on, and looking back on this first meeting with a man I would eventually call my friend, I am happy to report that I couldn't have been more wrong. Of course, Magadien wasn't there to kill me – even though he announced that to my colleagues, who were ready to take pictures and write the story for the following day's scoop. Besides, this was the *Daily Voice* newsroom and our currency was hyperbole.

My 2005 self was literally shaking in my shoes as I offered Magadien a smoke during that first meeting, which he accepted. Then he took me by surprise as he calmly introduced himself with a handshake. He went on to explain that he would have preferred that I called him first if I was going to write about him.

He was right; I was embarrassed. I had written a feature based on a documentary about his life. I could now see that a written account of what had played out in broadcast format wasn't the same. In fact, I had made it look far worse after it was dressed up in the *Daily Voice's* crazy headlines, subheads, captions and layout.

I apologised profusely to Magadien and I saved all his contact numbers. My fears about Magadien weren't misplaced. You see, Magadien Wentzel was the subject of a non-fiction book called *The Number*. *The Number*, by author Jonny Steinberg, broke all prison gang protocols as it revealed, through Magadien, the inner workings of a prison number gang. The crime of revealing the number gang's code not only guarantees the guilty party a dishonourable discharge, but also a death sentence.

In his rise to becoming a magistrate of the 28s prison gang, Magadien did some despicable things, including the ritual of 'taking blood'. His elevation in the gang ensured that his stint in Pollsmoor, one of the country's most notorious prisons for the number gangs, would be a lengthy one. Make no mistake: Magadien Wentzel was a bad man.

Magadien had had a difficult childhood that eventually led to a life of petty crime. Those petty crimes proved to be the gateway to a life behind bars that would see him more valued and respected inside prison than he ever was on the outside. That power was addictive. Inside prison he wielded authority.

But in 1999, all that would change, and Magadien's world view would change. A sudden act of God, so to speak, caused Magadien to want out of prison gang life. The price: death. Anyone who turns their back on their prison number gang is punished with death. But Magadien was prepared to live with the consequences.

On 25 August 1999, a tornado devastated Manenberg. Five people were killed, several people were wounded, and scores of houses and a school were destroyed. The people of Manenberg know death well because the area is notorious for gang murders. But this was different. This tornado left a trail of destruction in its wake – ironically skipping over the affluent suburbs as it built momentum before unleashing hell in that poor suburb in Cape Town.

I remember that day well. It was a Sunday – the start of my work week at the *Cape Times* as a junior freelance reporter. I got a call telling me not to come into the newsroom, but to go directly to Manenberg and meet up with photographer Peter Bauermeister. I knew the weather had been crazy the previous night, but I wasn't prepared for what I would see that morning in Manenberg. It was Armageddon, apocalypse, the aftermath of a powerful blast. The scene was chaotic – babies crying, people with their furniture packed on the pavement outside the ruins of brick and mortar. It was a desperate situation.

News of the tornado reached Pollsmoor, and Magadien remembers the frantic calls home and the relief when he was informed that, even though their house had been destroyed, his family was safe and had survived the freak storm. It was at that very moment that Magadien made a bold decision about the rest of his life. He knew he had been given a second chance. In 2003, he was released from Pollsmoor.

'I left drugs when I was in prison; that was when the tornado hit Manenberg in 1999. Our house was destroyed to the ground. But Allah gave me a chance. He didn't take my son and my wife at the time, and made me realise that life was short,' he later told me about that life-changing moment.

'I always thought that some mad guy out to get me would go after my family. That was my worst fear. And here comes a tornado and does it. So, I decided I had enough. I paid my dues to the number. I did everything for the number.'

What Magadien did next was unheard of in the world of prison gangs. He was about to turn his back on the gang and sign his own death warrant.

'I was in the top structure of the 28s gang. I don't even want to tell you my real rank, so I rather demote myself...but I was right up there. I was in the number for 22 years before giving it up.

'According to the number, I'm still in the number. But what I am saying is that I'm a reformed number, I'm a retired number. I'm not involved in the gang structure and I'm not involved in taking decisions. I've done what I've done.

'I could still get into trouble for turning my back on the number. Any day, a guy can walk up to me and put a gun to my head and end my life. But in the number, the high structure, there were mixed reactions. Some were glad, some were not so glad. Some said I'm selling out. Some said, "You had your time; we give you our blessing".'

Magadien then asked the head of prison, John Jansen, to put up a stage and provide a public address system to that he could speak to the members of all the prison gangs about his decision to leave the number. Jansen, who had begun a revolutionary programme to assist people like Magadien to reform, agreed.

'What I did next was to publicly give up my gang life – in front of all the 28s, all the 26s, all the 27s. I said, "Listen here, I'm stepping down. If you want to take me out, here I am now. Don't wait",' said Magadien.

If prison life was unforgiving, it had nothing on what awaited Magadien on the outside world. Outside prison, Magadien's status and former ranking as a leader of the 28s prison gang meant little, if nothing. He was just another unemployed middle-aged man with a prison record. And he was to find out just how harsh things were going to get. It was going to be like another prison sentence.

But Magadien was determined to seek redemption and to find a purpose for his life. He had something to offer and I would find that in his darkest moments his resolve would win out. He had a burning desire to be accepted into society and to live with dignity.

'I lived without dignity. I thought nothing of another person. I want to rectify that. I want dignity. I want to instill principles and values in my children and grandchildren. Not the principles and values that I lived by in the past, but the principles and values that need to be there for society to accept them – not as Magadien's children and grandchildren, but as members of society.'

But was it too late for Magadien to make amends?

Magadien decided that this path to redemption lay in reforming members of the number gang that he had had a hand in recruiting. If leaving the number gang was a death sentence, then this act was the final nail in the coffin. He had reasonable success. He believed those whom he had helped to reform responded to him because he spoke based on his life experience. But finding a way to structure his efforts was proving difficult, thanks to his criminal record and label as an ex-convict.

During this time, Magadien was also working with youth at risk. He tried coaching young footballers back in Manenberg, but this proved difficult too because of a lack of resources and equipment. The one thing going in his favour was that he was able to throw a successful Christmas party for the kids in Manenberg each year, because of the generous donations he received from individuals and business owners. Magadien was able to spread some much-needed cheer in a tough neighbourhood. Throughout the 14 years I've been his friend, he has never asked me for a single thing, except when it came to his Christmas party.

But the Magadien who walked into my office in July 2015 – a decade after I had first met him – was a broken man. He was skin and bones, he was battling with the after-effects of a bout of pneumonia that nearly killed him, and he looked defeated. He was living off instant noodles because that was all he could afford. Relations with his family had become difficult, as they had grown impatient with Magadien, who was sticking to his 'road less travelled' of seeking redemption. The easy road would have been to go back to prison and reclaim his power in the gang. But despite his setbacks, Magadien was still determined. But he was angry that, after 12 years, society wasn't ready to give him a chance.

'Everybody needs to put food on the table and that is what I've been struggling with for the past 12 years now: to be sustainable, to dress myself, to get medical treatment and food," Magadien said to me.

I was by now into my second stint as the editor of the *Cape Argus*. I remember feeling a sense of helplessness, listening to Magadien, and knowing how hard he had tried to make a difference over the years. It was mostly his selflessness that struck me.

'They know my history; my history is not a secret to anybody. My story was on TV; there was the book, The Number, and I was featured in newspapers. So, they know who I am,' he said.

'What makes me angry is that organisations invite me to speak, but then say they'll come back to me and see what they can do. I've been banging on their doors. Now I'm struggling for my grandchildren, walking my shoes broken for them. I did a programme for a Johannesburg organisation some years back and it was successful. But because of a lack of funding and the need in Joburg, my contract was terminated.

'I went back to the prisons to ask If I can help with the juveniles. Then I had to have a police clearance. But I come from that prison and told them they could log on to their computers and they could see I have a criminal record.'

Just a few days before my meeting with Magadien I encountered a man trying to assist a homeless man on a street corner in the Wynberg CBD. His face looked familiar and I realised it was Solly Staggie, brother of the late former Hard Livings gang leaders Rashied and Rashaad Staggie. Solly had served a 15-year sentence in jail and told me he was desperate to work to earn a living. But he complained that no one would give him a chance.

When I recounted this story to Magadien, he said: 'As Solly says, that is what we want. Society says we're sick and tired of you guys doing crime, getting involved in drugs and becoming druglords, and teaching children to abuse drugs and to participate in prostitution. We want to come out of that. 'But the same society is saying we want you to be a better person. I thought that was the honest truth. I grabbed it and thought here is my opportunity now. When I decided to change in prison, I was taught about what it means to have values and principles. I bought into that.

'But after 12 years, I've seen the opposite. I've been asking myself, "Why did I leave the gang?" I had everything. I could be the next high flyer. I was powerful, I was offered cars, houses, drugs, money. But because I believed change was possible, I rejected all those offers. I've been living on noodles for the past month. That's what I can afford. With God's grace, I have something in my stomach. Prison taught me how to discipline my stomach, so I'm used to that; but it's unhealthy.

'For me to find something sustainable is not about money. I don't want to become rich. I want to do what I love doing, and that is going to schools and talking to kids. The need is there. I've seen it. Kids don't go to school before they've had a slowboat (a dagga joint) and for me that is a concern. That is the generation that must take us forward – and they're dying. They're killing one another.'

But even at his lowest moment, Magadien was clear that he was not about to turn his back on the path he had chosen. His six grand-children had kept him motivated to live a crime-free life up until then. He had even tried to make amends to his victims, and took every opportunity to apologise for what he had done.

'I just want to say that I'm sorry. I can't take it back. I can't wipe it away. What I can do is ask them to find a small space in their hearts to see what I'm trying to achieve and just give me their blessing.

'I know what I did was wrong. Even in prison – the warders that I stabbed. I realise that doing wrong is wrong and you need to pay the price. What I don't understand is that I paid that price yet society, it seems, doesn't want to give me a chance.'

I do understand society's frustrations. In December 2019, Solly's brother, Rashied Staggie, was gunned down in London Road, Salt River. Rashied was brutally killed in a similar way to his twin brother Rashaad in 1996. A group calling themselves People Against Gangsterism and Drugs had marched to his house, and Rashaad was shot and set alight in London Road.

The twin brothers were inseparable when they ruled Manenberg and most of Cape Town's drug trade in the late 1980s and early 1990s.

They were the co-leaders of the Hard Livings gang, and their antics included driving down the streets of the suburb in their BMWs and passing wads of cash to people.

But Rashaad's murder made Rashied sing a different tune. Before and after going to prison for rape, Rashied used every opportunity to say that he was a changed man and even reborn as a Christian.

At the time of writing this, I still don't know who killed Rashied Staggie or why. As things go, that may never surface. What I do know is that it was a complicated matter. Rashied may well have been sincere about turning his life around; but I had spent enough time in visiting halls at prisons where he was incarcerated to understand what his wife and children meant to him.

But perhaps Rashied Staggie never had the resolve of a Magadien Wentzel. For what happened next for Magadien was nothing short of remarkable.

Around the same time as my last meeting with Magadien, I received a visit from an academic by the name of Brian Williams. Brian was about to launch a peace ambassadorship programme. The idea was that the peace ambassadors in Kensington and Factreton, in Cape Town, would be trained in conflict resolution skills and attempt to be a first line of defence for youth at risk of being recruited into gangs.

I then had a crazy idea. What if Magadien was trained as one of the 100 peace ambassadors, and spoke about his experiences as a member of prison gangs? Brian immediately took to the idea and promised to find Magadien, who had by then relocated to the Strand in order to recuperate from his illness. And that is where I left it.

True to his word, I would hear days later from Magadien that Brian had picked him up in the Strand, bought groceries for the household and made sure he attended the training sessions for the peace ambassadorship programme in Kensington and Factreton. As it turned out, Magadien proved to be a hit among his much younger peers. He had real practical experience with gangs and was very generous in sharing his knowledge.

Magadien graduated from the programme and I asked him what was next. But I'll admit that what he told me annoyed me at the time. Magadien had decided that there would be 99 skilled peace ambassadors to work with youth at risk in Kensington and Factreton.

Magadien had decided that he would put his skills to work with an intervention with homeless people in the Cape Town CBD. I remember feeling angry, frustrated and skeptical. I think I literally rolled my eyes; but I didn't share my apprehension with Magadien.

But yet again, I was wrong about Magadien. He was, as always, a few steps ahead of the rest of us.

The Magadien I spoke to in December 2016 – some 18 months after I saw him at his lowest point – had a spring in his step. His confidence was back. As we made our way to the famous Mariam's Kitchen across the road from the *Cape Argus* building in St George's Mall for breakfast, I complimented his red t-shirt with the large print of the crest of the famous football team we both love and support: Manchester United. As I ordered breakfast, he immediately started bantering with a few Liverpool fans because of his t-shirt. It was all friendly banter though, and I couldn't help thinking how, just 18 months ago, he might have withdrawn or have reacted very differently.

'When you introduced me to Brian Williams, I was very skeptical. People make promises and then they disappoint me. But, I thought, let me listen to what this guy has to say. He actually showed me quite the opposite. He kept his word and invited me to the peace-building training. At the end of the training, each of us had to select a project. I didn't know what to do. 'Most of the people were from the Factreton and Kensington area. I was the only person in the group from outside the area. I had to come up with a project that would benefit society and the people.

'I thought long and hard and then got a call from a woman from Khulisa Social Solutions in Joburg. She told me she had a colleague in Cape Town, Jesse Laitinen. I had a meeting with them and agreed to check it out, because I had nothing to lose by volunteering my services. 'I started facilitating some workshops for the homeless like peace building, anger management and restoring dignity. I was the new guy on the block and the guy that was in charge felt a bit threatened, because he thought I might come and take over his space.

'We got a contract from the City of Cape Town and were able to employ some people. I was asked to be a supervisor and thought it couldn't be that hard to supervise homeless people. My style differed from that of other supervisors: I would talk to them, didn't rush or threaten them and I listened to their stories to see where I could help.'

Magadien would run a highly successful veggie garden linked to the Service Dining Rooms in the Cape Town CBD, which fed homeless people while offering other support services. Khulisa Social Solutions had been offered a vacant piece of gravelled land next to the Fruit and Veg City store in Roeland Street. With Magadien in charge, the veggie garden was soon yielding produce that was sold to residents of the CBD, and this provided much-needed work opportunities for homeless people.

What was more, in an exciting turn of events, Magadien's fresh produce would end up on the plates of patrons of the top restaurants and hotels in the Cape Town CBD, as part of the social outreach projects of these establishments.

I didn't fully realise what Magadien was up to until I saw it for myself. Magadien had invited me to the Service Dining Rooms to have a chat about my role as a newspaper editor with a few of the homeless people he was working with.

I spoke very briefly about the *Cape Argus*, but I could tell that the newspaper meant very little to these marginalised citizens of our city. So I stopped talking, and listened instead. I suspect Magadien had planned it that way. I met the most remarkable group of homeless people, because I took a few minutes to just listen to them. How often had I refused to roll down my window to even just greet and acknowledge a homeless person asking for help at a traffic light?

But in this group, was a man who told of an unfortunate series of events that saw him end up in jail when it was completely unnecessary. Another was raising her baby on the streets and doing a fine job of it. There was the homeless BA Arts student, who took a lift from his campus in Gauteng and ended up in Cape Town, and who was creating incredible works of art on the streets.

At the end of these remarkable accounts of life on the streets, the leader of this collection of misfits gave me a knowing look. Magadien didn't have to say anything at that point, but I knew he was implying that I should do something. And that something was The Dignity Project.

And just like that, after years of struggle to find his purpose, Magadien had found redemption.

'I thought I should set the platform for them, so that they could show what they were capable of. I called in a few guests to speak to the group and expose them to people from all walks of life,' Magadien said.

'I brought you in; and out of that The Dignity Project was born. From there the project really grew because now people saw the homeless in a different light. They saw that people cared, and the project went from strength to strength.

'That was one of the things that I wanted to turn around. Why must people beg? It's not dignified to beg and it's not a nice thing. It's not a nice thing for people to have no shoes and no clothes. I know how that feels.

'When I was there – when I was released, as a changed man, society turned its back on me. There were a few individuals who I could call on and say I need this or that – but not for myself, for the projects I was involved in.'

With his newfound purpose, Magadien's health also improved. He looked younger, as if several burdens had been lifted from his shoulders. Relations with his family had improved too. Magadien beamed with pride when he spoke about his now seven grandchildren, although he worried about the eldest, who was at risk of being drawn into a gang.

The things he was saying now were very different to what he had been saying 18 months earlier.

'It's my approach to life. I don't believe in governmental laws. I hate it. I hate any law, except the universal law. Universal law says what goes up, must come down. If you put bad in, you get bad out. If you put good in, you get good out.

'It has nothing to do with religion – it is just life. What I'm putting in with my grandchildren – I am seeing the returns. It's not about buying expensive presents, but it's about making time for them.

'What makes me feel better is that when you are happy with what you are doing and you are doing positive things, then you become more positive. I wasn't in distress and I wasn't angry. As a matter of fact, I was happy.'

Life is still a challenge for Magadien, but he is looking forward and not back. When he turned his back on the gang, he signed his own death warrant, because it was an act that was punishable by death. But 18 months before our last chat, Magadien was more worried about dying of boredom. There is no danger of that now after he has tasted the rewards of devoting his life to the service of others. The past year has given him the self-belief that he can make a difference. But more importantly for his own sense of self-worth, he has realised that society needs him.

'My belief is that you can only release yourself from poverty if you give your children the opportunity to become successful. That is the key that will take you out of that hokkie[5] or crowded house,' he said.

'One thing that I can honestly say, is that 2016 was the best year of my life. For the first time, for one year, I could do good for a whole year – even if society didn't notice.

'One thing that I, Magadien, am proud of is that, for a year, I could dedicate my life in the service of the homeless and see how they grow, see how some of them change their ways, see how some of them move back to their families, and see how some of them – through my intervention – could reconcile with society.

'There are no words to comprehend how I feel. I proved yet again to society that I could make a difference if given the opportunity to engage.'

At the time of writing, Magadien was 59 years old and described himself as retired. He still throws a Christmas party for the kids of Manenberg every year and sends me a WhatsApp every now and then to ask me, 'Why are you so quiet?' In his own way, Magadien's resilience in seeking redemption can teach us all that determination and resolve for the right reasons will win the day.

FRIDAY FEBRUARY 27 2015   www.capeargus.co.za

Cape Argus

CAPE TOWN CYCLE TOUR

9 days to go

AM EDITION

R6.50
Country R6.50

9 771017 612005

MY INDEPENDENT APP   WANT NEWS ON YOUR MOBILE DEVICES? GET 4 WEEKS FREE!

Stolen baby found – 17 years later

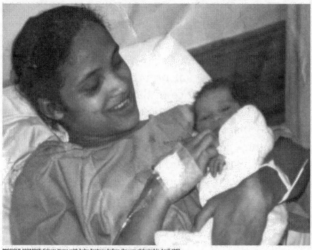

PRECIOUS MOMENT: Celeste Nurse with baby Zephany before she was abducted in April 1997.

Hawks arrest suspect in 1997 Groote Schuur abduction of Zephany Nurse

Chelsea Geach
STAFF REPORTER
chelsea.geach@inl.co.za

AN ASTONISHING coincidence has led to the discovery of Zephany Nurse – stolen from her mother's arms in Groote Schuur Hospital as a newborn 17 years ago.

A DNA test has confirmed that Zephany, now in matric at a Cape Town school, is the daughter of Celeste and Morné Nurse, who lost their three-day-old daughter when she was snatched from her sleeping mother's arms in her hospital bed in April 1997.

Now a 50-year-old woman has been arrested by the Hawks. She is to appear in the Cape Town Magistrate's Court today.

Celeste and Morné Nurse, who went on to have three more children, have celebrated Zephany's birthday every year since, never giving up hope that their first-born would come back to them someday.

Zephany grew up with a different name, and a different family, never knowing she was not their real daughter. But last month her biological sister, Cassidy Nurse, started Grade 8 at the same school that Zephany attended, and fellow pupils noticed a startling resemblance she bore to a matric pupil.

When Cassidy told her parents about the matric girl, hope began to strengthen in their hearts after 17 long years.

> "CELESTE AND MORNE NURSE NEVER GAVE UP HOPE THEIR FIRST-BORN WOULD COME BACK TO THEM SOMEDAY"

The Nurses invited the matric girl for a cup of coffee, under the pretence that they wanted to meet Cassidy's friend. When they too saw the striking similarities between the girls, Morné Nurse contacted the police.

Soon the Hawks were involved, questioning the girl's parents and taking DNA samples.

Police spokesman Lieutenant-Colonel André Traut confirmed last night that a woman, 50, had been arrested yesterday morning.

The woman and her husband, in his fifties, have no other children.

"The suspect is being charged with kidnapping, fraud and contravening

To page 3

NEWS
Cycle Tour pullout today

LIFE
Designer for the dead

Page 17

FRIDAY FILES
Pioneering 'Hell Driver'

Page 15

27 February 2015. The *Cape Argus* front page on the day the missing child Zephany Nurse was found – 17 years after she was stolen from her mother's hospital bedside when she was just a few days old. ©*Independent Media*

4 Missing

Every year, for 17 years, a Cape Town family celebrated the birthday of their daughter with a special cake donated by Pick n Pay and the *Cape Argus* taking a picture for publication. Why was this a story for the city's big daily newspaper, you may ask? That's because the Nurse family had last seen their daughter Zephany, when she was just three days old.

Zephany was stolen from her sleeping mother's hospital room by a woman posing as a nurse on 30 April 1997. I always wondered what went through the minds of her parents, Celeste and Morné Nurse, when they posed for that picture for the *Cape Argus*, trying to put on a brave face. Where was Zephany? What did she look like? Was she being cared for? Was she trafficked out of the country? Was she even alive?

On 29 April 2011, *Cape Argus* reporter Esther Lewis reported:

'ZEPHANY Nurse has just turned 14, a day marked every year by her parents and three younger siblings. Yet she has never been present for any of the parties.

'Tomorrow is 14 years since Zephany was snatched from Groote Schuur Hospital when she was just three days old. Her mother Celeste remembered a woman dressed in a nurse's outfit holding the baby, but fell asleep soon afterwards because of her pain medication.

'When she awoke, her baby was missing.

'Police investigations into the disappearance are now being handled by the organised crime unit.

'In July 2009, the Nurse family received an anonymous phone call from a woman who claimed she had information about Zephany.

'She wanted R5 000 for her help.

'The woman never showed up, but Glenda Doubell – who lived in the same street as the child's grandmother – was arrested and confessed to the prank call.

'She was fined R5 000 and ordered to do 300 hours of community service, along with three years of house arrest.

'Yesterday the girl's parents, Celeste and Morné, along with their three children, Micah, 3, Joshua, 5, and Cassidy, 10, honoured her birthday.

'The three children have never met Zephany, but they all know about their older sister, and that she was kidnapped.

'Celeste said the tragedy had resulted in her being overprotective of her other three children, who, she said, she never let out of her sight.

'She said they often asked why they could not ride their bicycles around the corner in their gated community. She explained to them that children get kidnapped, and she did not want anything to happen to them.

'When Celeste woke up yesterday morning, she reminded Morné to wish Zephany a happy birthday.

'Each year, Pick n Pay in Constantia supplies the family with a birthday cake for the missing girl.

'This year it was a huge chocolate cake. "Happy Birthday Zephany, we miss you", the fresh cream letters read.

"We do this every year to show that we haven't forgotten about her," said Morné.

'In his heart, he believes that she is safe, happy and being well cared for.

'Even though 14 years have passed, Celeste still feels the bond to her daughter.

"There was a smell on her when she was born. I smelled it the other day. I still feel our connection."

'Morné and Celeste said faith and hope were what had carried them through the years.

'Celeste said that she forgave the person who took her child a long time ago.

"So now the only decent thing she can do is bring her back home. It's been long enough," she pleaded.'

It was agonising for the Nurses not knowing. Usually, when a child goes missing, particularly in the Western Cape, the chances are high that the child will be found dead after being raped. This was the reality that I witnessed for so many families across the Cape Flats over my more than 20 years in various newsrooms across the city. It is a brutal situation, and I can't imagine the trauma these families go through. Or, in the case of Celeste and Morné Nurse, the trauma of just not knowing. The only photograph they had of her was one taken when she was just a few hours old.

It was around 2005, when I had the idea to do a special feature on all the missing children in the Western Cape, and why it was especially such a phenomenon on the Cape Flats. The *Daily Voice* was the perfect vehicle, and we splashed the faces of missing children across the front page of the tabloid newspaper. I was disappointed that it didn't have the desired reaction that I was looking for, i.e. for both the public and the authorities to step up efforts to find the missing children. And this was despite the fact that there were literally hundreds of missing kids on the Cape Flats at any given time.

It made me think about how the British press was covering the Madeleine McCann story, a little girl who had gone missing in Spain, at the time. One child. One child too many, in their view. And rightfully so. Were we just desensitised? It was going to take some shock and awe to get folks out of their comfort zone, I thought.

My missing children project led me to another heartbreaking account of a little boy who appeared to have vanished into thin air right in front of his house in Mitchells Plain while outside, attending to his daily chores. Matthew Ohlsson was just nine years old when he went missing.

Matthew's mom Michelle Ohlsson is one of the bravest women I have ever met. She started an initiative called 'Concerned Parents of Missing Children'. They would kick down the doors of drug dens if they needed to find missing children. Michelle and her husband Michael also opened their home in Mitchells Plain to foster children.

In 2018, Matthew would have celebrated his 30th birthday. Genevieve Serra, intrepid journalist and former colleague at the *Daily Voice*, reported the event on 26 February 2018 as follows:

'The family of Matthew Ohlsson, who disappeared when he was just nine years old, held a party for what would have been his 30th birthday on Saturday.

'His family do not believe Matthew is dead, and his parents, Michael and Michelle Ohlsson, say they are no longer searching for a little boy, but for a man with a flower-shaped birthmark on his chest.

'The family had a birthday cake with Matthew's face printed on it, and read through old newspaper articles written when he first disappeared. Matthew, a pupil at Westville Primary School, had gone to fetch the wheelie bin outside their home in Delheim Close, Westridge on 24 March 1997, and was never seen again.

'Michelle says he was barefoot, dressed in his underpants, and a green and grey vest which had 'USA' printed on it. Police had offered a R50 000 reward for any information leading to finding Matthew and even called in the army to assist with the search.

'The mother believes her young son would only have gone away with someone whom he knew.

'Speaking of her heartache of dealing with her loss over the years, Michelle tells the *Daily Voice*: "What I am aiming for is peace of mind, and to have an answer of what happened to my child. I don't believe he is dead. I don't feel any death; without a body, there is no death in my soul.

"I am going to do whatever I have to do to find out what happened to my child. Today's party is not in memory of him, but in honour that we believe he is still alive."

'Michelle says Matthew was a helpful boy "with a bit of a temper" and loved to mimic his dad.

"Matthew was a handyman just like his father and he was a determined little boy."

'She says on that fateful day, the family had been preparing for a visit to her sister in Lavender Hill, but changed their plans when Michael was delayed.

"I told my children to get undressed, so Matthew was not dressed to go out," she explains.

'After his disappearance, the couple started fostering children. They also founded the organisation Concerned Parents of Missing Children, and formed relationships with the parents of other missing kids on the Cape Flats.

'Michelle says they will never give up hope of finding Matthew.

"He is now 30 years old. When I thought about it, I came to realise we are not looking for that little boy anymore. We are looking for a grown man who has a flower birthmark on his chest."

'Michael says they've followed up on all leads, but many calls turned out to be hoaxes.

"I even went as far as Strand because they believed they had found Matthew," he says. "But it was not him, it was a boy who looked like Matthew."

'Mitchells Plain mom Joanie Lucas, the mother of Anastacia Lucas, who disappeared 21 years ago, at the age of seven, was also invited to the party. Little Anastacia went missing while playing at a park near her Westridge home. She was never found.'

For some parents, the torture of having a child go missing is short-lived. There are more names than I care to remember in stories that I covered of young children, who hadn't even reached their pre-teen years, but who were found murdered – often after being raped – just days after going missing. This is a particular affliction on the Cape Flats.

What always struck me while interviewing the parents of these missing or dead children was how they managed to retain their dignity despite their pain and suffering. I remember my toddler daughter going walkabout in a store in a busy mall for a split second once and how I lost my mind. I don't think I'd be able to remain composed if it happened to me. I always thought I would kick down doors and would probably get myself killed trying to find my child. I'm not for one moment suggesting these parents of missing children could have done that. But it always got me thinking: where is the Madeleine McCann-type anger and the response from the media?

My missing children project led me to the Greater Blue Downs area along the R300 highway to the north of Cape Town, and a whole new can of worms that was later dubbed 'The Bush of Evil'.

The Community Policing Forum chairperson of the Greater Blue Downs had a furious work ethic, especially since this was very much a part-time and voluntary job, but also a fantastic relationship with the management of the Kleinvlei Police Station. Malvern de Bruyn knew everything and everyone in the Delft, West Bank, Blue Downs, Blackheath and Eersterivier communities.

Malvern took me to a massive expanse of bush the size of several rugby fields. The bush either surrounded these suburbs or was found smack bang in a neighbourhood where there should have been a municipal play park. What was bad was that the bush wasn't even indigenous like fynbos or something that the greenies would believe was worth fighting for. What was worse was that the bush area was often used as a thoroughfare by residents. What was despicable was that the bush was used as perfect cover for rapes and robberies, and as a dumping ground for murderers to leave bodies. Many of those bodies were those of tiny children – many of whom would not reach their 10th birthday. What was unforgiveable was that Malvern, his colleagues and the police had advocated for years to have the bush cut down – but to no avail.

And so, the Bush of Evil was born in the *Daily Voice* – followed by an editorial campaign that would eventually make the public and the authorities sit up and take notice. Malvern took me around to the parents, often single moms, whose children had been murdered and the bodies dumped in the bushes. It was heart-wrenching stuff and was splashed across the cover and inside pages of the *Daily Voice* under the headline 'The Bush of Evil'.

Karl Brophy, my Irishman editor at the time, reminded me that, if I wanted to make an impact, I was going to have to be relentless. I spent days and weeks in the Greater Blue Downs area doing follow-up stories. It got a rise from the public, but no action yet from the City of Cape Town. Their comment was simply that the foliage anchored down the shifting sand in the area. It was a cold and callous response in the face of the trauma the community was suffering.

It was time to ramp things up. The problem was that the tabloid master, Karl, was abroad when my missing children campaign needed momentum. He had given me a book to read called 'The Insider'. It was a memoir by former *Daily Mirror* editor Piers Morgan – complete with a collection of front pages showing how he had handled some of the campaigns that the British tabloid had undertaken. At the time, the paper was dead against sending British troops to war in Iraq, and his stance eventually got Morgan fired. I remember walking to my flat to get the book, because I'd seen something that gave me an idea that would get the attention of the mayor of Cape Town at the time, Nomaindia Mfeketo.

It was a front page that was stark in its simplicity. A black and white image of then UK Prime Minister, Tony Blair, set against a black background, with both his hands in front of his chest and palms facing outwards. Blood had been photoshopped onto his hands. The headline screamed, 'Blood on his hands'.

Morgan was a master of the dramatic effect. There was a dotted line where readers could cut out the front page and an entry form-like box that readers could complete, sign and then send back to the newspaper. Morgan had turned the front page of the *Daily Mirror* into a petition that called on the government to refrain from sending British troops into Iraq for what he regarded as an unjust war.

The stand-in editor and page 1 layout designer, Nic Naude, loved it. What was important was that the *Daily Mirror* front page worked. There was no reason to re-invent the wheel. The talented Nic ordered the picture desk to get him a similar image of Mfeketo with her hands out. A tough ask, and we may have to go out to get one, I thought. But the picture desk duo of Leon Müller and Noor Slamdien always delivered.

The following day the petition front page created a stir. There was a picture of Mayor Mfeketo with blood on her hands because of her administration's inaction in not cutting down the Bush of Evil. The campaign was renamed Kill the Bush. Soon Kill the Bush had taken on a life of its own – complete with a logo. My missing children project finally had the momentum it needed.

The response was unprecedented. Our mailroom was overflowing with signed petitions from thousands of readers demanding that the Bush of Evil be cut down. The newsdesk was inundated with calls from residents in the Greater Blue Downs area with their own stories of how they had been hit by crime in the Bush of Evil. The Bush of Evil became a discussion point on radio stations and the City of Cape Town was increasingly pressured to respond. Of course, the *Daily Voice* 'made a meal' out of delivering the thousands of petitions to the doorstep of the mayor at the civic centre, with another big front-page splash.

Days later, we had success. I received a breathless call from an excited Malvern de Bruyn, informing me that I should come through to the area because workmen from the city had arrived to start cutting down the bush. Wow, a bit of advocacy journalism was all that was needed after all.

We all knew that cutting down the bush wouldn't serve as an antidote to the rampant crime, especially the most heinous crimes of child rape and murder. These were societal challenges that needed more than a quick fix. But cutting down the bush would at least get rid of the cover for the evil perpetrators who were committing these horrific acts in broad daylight.

But the Greater Blue Downs area wasn't the only part of Cape Town where the alien and invasive Port Jackson plants that make up the Bush of Evil grew abundantly and covered vast expanses of land. There are huge tracts of land in Mitchells Plain and Philippi that have a Bush of Evil of its own. It makes sense why the town planners at the time wanted to plant Port Jackson plants, when Mitchells Plain was designed for people who were violently kicked out of their homes in areas that were declared whites only areas under apartheid's Group Areas Act. The plant is like a weed that spreads quickly, doesn't need much water and can grow in soil that resembles beach sand. These apartheid town planners didn't foresee the unintended consequence: a hunting and burial ground for one of South Africa's most notorious serial killers.

I grew up in a part of Mitchells Plain called Lentegeur. I have happy childhood memories of Salie Street. Well, mostly. It was in Salie Street, as a six-year-old, that I decided to become a reporter. It happened one night when a father came home from work and found his two young sons playing outside their house located in a corner of our cul-de-sac. Apparently, well according to the nosy next door neighbour who sold fish, he found his wife with another man. He picked up a length of wrought-iron that was popular at the time for making burglar bars and proceeded to kill them both with several blows. He made a run for it and was never seen again. Rumour has it that he moved abroad. (Chillingly, his name was also Gasant.)

But what I remember very clearly about that night in 1984 was the news reporters and photographers at the scene in our little cul-de-sac. One of them was interviewing the fish-selling next-door neighbour.

The flash from a press camera. The TV crew. That was what I wanted to do, I decided.

What I also remember very fondly about Salie Street and Lentegeur was how I could get around with my mates on our BMX bicycles. I had a red one that had a 'Cheetah' sticker on the frame and I could ride that bike as fast as a cheetah could run. Or, at least, that is how it felt.

One of the areas we frequented with our bikes was called Die Heuwels (The Hills). It was located directly above Salie Street and it was an area our parents warned us to stay away from. We had the most fantastic adventures in the Port Jackson bushes that covered Die Heuwels.

But in 1986, two years before our family moved out of Mitchells Plain, a savage crime spree began that was attributed to just one killer. A serial killer. The Station Strangler would eventually be credited with the murders of 22 young boys. At our school, we were warned about the killer and our parents were on heightened alert. Especially, because Die Heuwels was one of the areas that the Station Strangler operated in. But boys will be boys. Of course, we went back to Die Heuwels to ride our bikes. When I tell my mom about it now, she still shudders.

The modus operandi of the killer was to prey on young pre-teen boys and lure them away from cafés and games arcades near train stations. He would then rape them, strangle them, and dump their bodies in a shallow grave. His behaviour bore the classic traits of a serial killer who left clues, wanted to be caught and wanted to be a media sensation. And it worked. Some of the country's best detectives were assigned to the case, and some newspapers at the time, like the *Cape Argus*, even had a graphic that was pinned to Station Strangler stories. There was mass hysteria about the killings – particularly in Mitchells Plain, even though some killings outside the area were credited to the Station Strangler – and for good reason.

Almost eight years and 22 bodies later, police cracked the case. Norman Afzal Simons, a teacher who worked and lived in Mitchells Plain, was arrested. Simons was eventually convicted of only the murder of 10-year-old Elroy van Rooyen, which happened outside of Mitchells Plain, in an area called Melton Rose, near Eersterivier. Bush of Evil territory. In 1995, Simons was convicted of the murder of Elroy van Rooyen and sentenced to 35 years in jail. There was a DNA match in the killing, but Simons could not be linked to the other 21 murders. Even so, he was branded the Station Strangler.

It was neat. Simons was arrested just ahead of South Africa's first democratic elections in 1994. The National Party, who had ruled for many years under apartheid, claimed his arrest as a victory and that law and order could be entrusted to the party that had oppressed those very same people for decades. It appeared to have worked, because the National Party retained power in Mitchells Plain and the Cape, while the former liberation movement, the ANC, was triumphant everywhere else in South Africa.

One man who didn't believe that Simons was the serial killer that the police had sought was a man called Koos Louw. He was an advocate who had first represented Simons, and again a few decades later, when there was a court inquest into the other 21 murders. Now Koos didn't make his doubts known just because that is what lawyers do when defending their clients in the press. Koos really believed – and he would tell you so, and why, during private conversations. In fact, he believed with such conviction that Simons wasn't the Station Strangler that he swore an oath to grow his hair and only cut it once Simons was cleared of being the serial killer.

For Koos, there were just too many anomalies. For one, the DNA evidence of the other cases was stashed away in Pretoria, and was never made available to him. There were other rapes and murders of young boys after Simons was jailed. It was possible that these were copycat killers. But most pertinently for Koos was that there were two adults still living in Mitchells Plain. As young boys, they had claimed that they had escaped the Station Strangler, and they had described a distinctly different-looking man. They had been approached by a man who had asked them to help him carry boxes of bananas to his car, but the two boys became suspicious and ran away.

Koos made it his life's work to prove Simons was innocent of the other murders. Unfortunately, he passed away a few years ago and Simons remains incarcerated.

At least, with Simons locked away, the parents of the other 21 Station Strangler victims have answers – albeit that his guilt in their murders was contested by Koos Louw. Imagine the agony and distress of parents whose children never came home – not knowing whether they were dead or alive. What were they like as adults? Did they have children and families of their own? Michelle Ohlsson will never know this about her Matthew.

But on 26 February 2015, something unexpected happened that no one could have anticipated. The *Cape Argus* newsroom was abuzz as reporter Chelsea Geach put together a front page lead splash that, as editor of the paper at the time, I thought was just too good to be true.

Zephany Nurse had been found 17 years after being snatched from her mom in Groote Schuur Hospital. The picture in the paper of her on her next birthday would actually have her in it, I thought. It was a goosebump moment and we couldn't believe our ears. Even veterans in the newsroom, like our Back Desk Editor, Viv Horler – who had by then seen, done and reported on it all – was gobsmacked. Viv had lived through the Zephany Nurse case from the start, and would now witness its conclusion. That night in the newsroom, we all knew it was a once-in-a-lifetime story.

There was an image of Zephany's mom, Celeste Nurse, holding her newborn in her arms in the *Cape Argus* on 27 February 2015. The accompanying front page lead by Chelsea read:

'An astonishing coincidence has led to the discovery of Zephany Nurse – stolen from her mother's arms in Groote Schuur Hospital as a newborn 17 years ago.

'A DNA test has confirmed that Zephany, now in matric at a Cape Town school, is the daughter of Celeste and Morné Nurse, who lost their 3-day-old daughter when she was snatched from her sleeping mother's arms in her hospital bed in April 1997.

'Now a 50-year-old woman has been arrested by the Hawks. She was to appear in the Cape Town Magistrate's Court on Friday.

'The parents, who went on to have three more children – Cassidy, Joshua and Micah – have celebrated Zephany's birthday every year since, never giving up hope that their first-born would come back to them someday.

'Zephany grew up with a different name, and a different family, never knowing she was not their real daughter.

'But last month her biological sister, Cassidy Nurse, started Grade 8 at the same school that Zephany attended, and fellow pupils noticed a startling resemblance she bore to a matric pupil.

'When Cassidy told her parents about the matric girl, hope began to strengthen in their hearts after 17 long years.

'The Nurses invited the matric girl for a cup of coffee, under the pretense that they wanted to meet Cassidy's friend.

'When they too saw the striking similarities between the girls, Morné Nurse contacted the police.

'Soon the Hawks were involved, questioning the girl's parents and taking DNA samples.

'Police spokesman, Lieutenant-Colonel André Traut, confirmed on Thursday night that a woman had been arrested on Thursday.

'"The suspect is being charged with kidnapping, fraud and contravening sections 32 (4) (a) and (b) of the Children's Act – in that she fraudulently pretended that she was the biological mother of a child," Traut said.

'"The kidnapped girl has since been placed in the care of the Department of Social Services of the Western Cape government."

'Without knowing it, Celeste and Morné Nurse had been living within a few kilometres of their daughter.

'As the years went by, they celebrated Zephany's birthday on April 28 each year, often with a giant cake sponsored by Pick n Pay.

'And they kept searching.

'In a 2010 interview with the *Weekend Argus*, Morné said he was still holding out for his lost daughter.

'"I'll never, ever give up hope. I can feel it in my gut – my daughter is out there and she is going to come home."

'But last night, he was not willing to speak to the media as the family met to decide the way forward now that Zephany had been found and her future thrown into turmoil.

'"We have no closure here," he said.'

Chelsea had it spot on. There was turmoil. What happens when a missing child snatched as a newborn is found almost two decades later? The hopes of a happy ending for the Nurse family were soon dashed. Also that of the editorial team at the *Cape Argus*, who had so faithfully taken a picture at Zephany's 'birthday' each year. A protracted and complicated court case played out involving the woman who had stolen Zephany. There was a blow-by-blow account of every moment of the case in the media and the young girl (ironically) had to turn to the courts in a bid to protect her given identity – the only identity she had known her entire life.

Lavona Solomon was eventually convicted of kidnapping and is serving a 10-year sentence.

Was the finding of Zephany Nurse a happy ending? Hardly. She had forged a bond with the 'mother' who had stolen her and her husband. That family was broken apart too, as the husband, Michael Solomon, would learn of the despicable crime his wife had committed.

By this time, the Nurses were also a family torn apart. Details of both Morné and Celeste's personal life and relationships became fair game in the media. And the media spotlight was never far behind for Zephany Nurse either, as later still, the spotlight fell on the reality that she had a strained relationship with her biological parents.

She later revealed her identity as Miche Solomon, which she had earlier asked the court to protect. She also published a book, in which she provided intimate details of her feelings about her biological parents and the couple that had cared for her and loved her for most of her life. But the media glare picked apart her every move. Writing the book was a money-making scheme, one newspaper even opined.

One of the non-profit organisations doing advocacy work in the area of missing children brings the issue into stark perspective on its website:

'A child goes missing every five hours in South Africa, according to figures released by the South African Police Service Missing Persons Bureau for 2013. This adds up to a total of 1697 children. Fortunately, 77% of children are found, according to Missing Children South Africa's statistics. Sadly, this still leaves us with at least 23% of the missing children not being located.'

Perhaps one day there will be a happy ending for Zephany Nurse and her biological family. For now, it is too complex a situation to contemplate a reunion with a family she never had a bond with. With the only real mother she knew in jail, it is a situation almost too ghastly to contemplate.

As ghastly as never finding a missing child? Or a missing child ending up murdered?

It is a comparison and a choice no parent should have to make.

role is to support the restitution process through ongoing memory work with residents. In this process 'the return' to District Six is a form of activism – an reclaiming a part of the city that was once home, and an acknowledgment of c loss of community. We try [...] iple narrative approach to represent t work to the public and f[...] ites in the area.

The questions now fac[...] e Museum are:
• How do we memori[...]
• How do we rebuild a[...]
• Once new homes are [...] ry of the empty site is lost, will we the historical memory [...] ed removals?

Our work with these ques[...] nd happens alongside the redevelopm process.

23 January 2020. Bonita Bennett was the Director of the District Six Museum for 11 years before stepping down from the position in January 2020. She says she joined the District Six Museum because she was drawn to people's stories. ©*ANA Pictures*

5 *Gentrification*

I grew up in a part of Woodstock, near central Cape Town, that wasn't exactly an area that would fetch you a fortune when you re-sold your house. But my 10-year-old self was pretty excited at the prospect of moving so close to the city and out of Mitchells Plain. So were my parents. Remember, this was 1988 and the Station Strangler was still looming large in Mitchells Plain.

My dad, a truck driver, and my mom, a sample seamstress, had a modest income, but they wanted only the best for us. So, Woodstock it was. The house in Essex Street was a bit of a dump when we first moved in, with broken floors, holes in the walls and a pest problem. But, with a little bit of TLC, my folks quickly brought it up to a decent standard. And more importantly, we would all have our own rooms. The old house in Salie Street, Mitchells Plain, had just three bedrooms. I shared a room with my sister and my two older siblings shared a room.

The double-storey house cost just R38 000 at the time – a steal. But here's the rub: even though all the neighbours were coloured at the time, the area was still classified as a whites-only area. In addition to signing what seemed like thousands upon thousands of documents, my dad needed to apply for a permit to buy the house, because he was a coloured man. He was prepared to suffer the humiliation in the interests of providing us with a better life.

But just days into settling into our new home, it became evident that Woodstock had problems of its own. Chiefly, a drug problem. On either side of our house and across the road were what was known as smokkelhuise. Drug dens. They sold weed and mandrax mainly. Later they sold rocks.[6]

Also, the gang activity in Woodstock was far more sophisticated than in Mitchells Plain, with gang members having access to guns and other resources. We were four children and, as fate would have it, one of my siblings would succumb to an addiction that would last almost two decades. It was inevitable, but if you looked at it in the cold light of day, a rate of 1 out of 4 wasn't awful. His addiction led to theft to feed his habit, and his involvement with some shady characters. But I'm happy to report that he's been clean for a good few years now.

But, despite the problems, we were happy. I made some lifelong friendships in Woodstock and navigated my way through school and eventually my journalism studies while living in the suburb. It was close to everything that was cool for a young person growing up in Cape Town.

I got a big news scoop while living in Woodstock too, as a 20-year-old upstart journalist. I was desperately trying to break into the freelance journalism game in Cape Town after a successful one-year internship at *The Star* in Johannesburg. It was late on a Saturday afternoon and there was a thunderous sound. Instinctively, I grabbed my camera and ran towards the general area I thought it had emanated from.

My instincts were spot on. A car explosion had been detonated just outside the Woodstock Police Station. The car was still burning when I arrived and I got some pretty decent images. Remember, this was 1999 and the height of the so-called urban terror attacks in Cape Town. They were blamed on the group known as People Against and Gangsterism and Drugs, or Pagad.

Soon, the media scrum arrived. But by then the picture opportunities were pretty static, with only the charred remains of the car to be seen - the flames long extinguished by firefighters. I spotted a familiar face in the crowd. It was the famous press photographer Benny Gool, and I told him I had some images he would be interested in. During the fleeting conversation, he asked me not to speak to anyone else. The following Monday, my picture was splashed across the front page of the *Cape Times* with my accompanying front page lead. When I was later asked how much I wanted for the pictures and my story, my answer was simple: a permanent job!

As it later became known in the neighbourhood that I was a journalist, I always had the sense that the characters linked to gangs like the Junior Mafias and The Rich Kids (who specialised in burglaries of high-end properties in affluent suburbs) were very cautious of me. But I made a pact with myself never to write about things too close to home. It's expressed colloquially as 'not kakking[7] on your own stoep', I suppose.

Years later, after we all got married or settled down and moved out of the house, my parents felt the five-bedroom house was too hard for them to maintain, as they were approaching retirement age. They sold it for just R150 000 in the early 2000s.

Now, when I drive around the lower part of Woodstock, I hardly recognise it. Our old double storey house in Essex Street could now easily sell for a cool R3-million. So, what has changed? It was on the verge of being an inner-city slum area but has become one of the most sought-after areas in the city.

In a word: gentrification. It's not as brutal as apartheid's Group Areas Act era, when entire communities were bulldozed out of their neighbourhood – like District Six – and dumped on the desolate Cape Flats. But it may as well be. Little by little, communities and their traditions are gobbled up in the name of market forces and development. It's probably inevitable, too, and happens to suburbs all over the world as global citizens become more mobile, want to be closer to their places of work, and have foreign cash to spend.

Gentrification is what happens when members of communities are lured by the promise of selling their property to greedy developers. In the beginning, it all seems good and well, because the riff-raff is seemingly weeded out. But as the property prices increase, so do the rates. And soon, little by little, the original residents move out because the area just becomes too expensive to live in.

Soon the complexion of the entire suburb changes. Soon, the Kaapse Klopse[8] are indulged rather than embraced in the Bo-Kaap, where their famous mockery of slave bosses was first performed, and in District Six at the turn of the 20th century. Soon, someone who moved into District Six just five years ago will complain about the Muslim call to prayer that has been performed for a hundred years. This is not an exaggeration: it really happened.

During Ramadan (Islam's holiest month) in 2019, I was shocked to read a tweet about the City of Cape Town investigating a noise complaint against the Muir Street Mosque over its athaan – the Muslim call to prayer. A resident, who had moved in five years earlier, complained about the call to prayer. A single complaint that the City

of Cape Town said it was obliged to investigate – even though the
City knew the significance of the mosque and its special place in the
history of District Six.

The mosque has a grand tradition – along with the Moravian
Church, the Aspeling Street Mosque and a few schools – because it is
all that remains of the vibrant community that was once District Six.
Children of all religions stopped playing in the street and ran inside
when the sunset athaan (known as Maghrib) was made. The Muir
Street Mosque was 100 years old in 2019.

The City of Cape Town should have told this new resident to get
stuffed. But investigate the complaint they did. They sent two rep-
resentatives to the mosque to measure the decibel level of the call to
prayer. It was found to be way below the level of a noise complaint.
But instead of dismissing the misguided complaint out of hand, it
was downgraded to a nuisance complaint. It was ludicrous. Imagine
moving to Istanbul and filing a complaint with the city's authorities
about the 5 500 mosques making athaan five times a day? They would
laugh it off!

I tweeted about it and my tweet went viral. People from all walks of
life, from every religion, and even agnostics, pledged their support for
the Muir Street Mosque. It soon became a major story in the news media.
Even then recently-retired Western Cape Premier, Helen Zille, tweeted
her support with the message, 'Hands off Muir Street Mosque'.

I reached out to the Sheikh of the mosque, and soon I was playing
a clandestine advisory role to the mosque committee on how to
proceed in the public domain. An online petition was started by
someone unknown to the mosque and close to 100 000 people signed
it. I advised the committee to flip the switch and to make their fight
against the complaint more than just about the Muir Street Mosque.
There were other suburbs where the athaan had already been
outlawed because of the City of Cape Town's noise by-law. A famous
church in Paarl, that had been there for more than 100 years, was also
prevented from ringing its church bells.

Now let me put this noise by-law into perspective. It is complete
nonsense. The same by-law states that dog owners will be fined if the
animal barks incessantly for more than two minutes. That by-law led
to a blind busker at St Georges Mall, who had been there for more

than a decade, being roughed up and manhandled by the City of Cape Town's law enforcement unit because of a complaint.

The strategy I put to the mosque committee was to treat the noise complaint as a sideshow to a bigger malaise. I encouraged the mosque committee to tackle the by-law itself and to call for all calls to prayers, like the athaan and the ringing of church bells, to be exempt from the noise by-law. While they were doing so, they should continue to make the athaan. It worked and the Mayor of Cape Town, Dan Plato, let me know through an official that the athaan would never be stopped while he was in charge of the city.

In the context of District Six, it was a tiny victory, however. A famous line in the award-winning *District Six – The Musical*, by the late Taliep Petersen and David Kramer, has a blind man character called 'Ta Makkah. As the bulldozers move in quite late into the musical, 'Ta Makkah proclaims that the land will forever be cursed. The blind character may have been spot on about that. After the monstrosity that was then the Cape Technikon was built on a small part of the land, the bigger part that was once filled with homes remained vacant for almost 30 years before only a handful of land claimants, some of the original residents of District Six, were brought back to a tiny stretch of land across the road from the Muir Street Mosque. For the most part, the area is a gravelled wasteland in a prime location in Cape Town. And successive governments in the Western Cape, under both the ANC and the DA, have failed to do anything meaningful to restore justice. Again, market forces rule. Many of the original residents who had filed a land claim have since passed on.

There have been token gestures, like replacing the new name (Zonnebloem) with the original name of District Six. Keizergracht Street has been renamed Hanover Street – the latter a famous landmark in the old, vibrant suburb. But nothing meaningful has happened on 'Ta Makkah's cursed land. As a young TV reporter for the recently launched free-to-air broadcaster's news show *eNews*, in the early 2000s, I was excited to report that thousands of former District Six residents would soon be moving back. I was honoured to report such a historic announcement; but it was an announcement that turned out to be a lie.

During my time at the *Cape Argus* writing weekly profiles on interesting individuals for the 'Friday Files', I interviewed Bonita Bennett, Director of the District Six Museum, on the occasion of the 50th anniversary of the apartheid government declaring District Six a whites-only area (on 11 February 1966). Bonita herself had fond memories of District Six as a child in its heyday. But what she subsequently told me surprised me in a way I had not expected. She said the families of many of the people so violently forced out of District Six were reporting that they had died of a broken heart. Died of a broken heart? That couldn't be, my journalist head told me. But my heart started thinking differently.

Before interviewing Bonita, I took a picture of the plaque outside the museum – the building that used to be the old Methodist Church. In that very church, Bishop Peter Storey had delivered fierce anti-apartheid sermons from the pulpit. The plaque was engraved with Bishop Storey's words: 'All who pass by remember with shame the many thousands of people who lived for generations in District Six and other parts of the city and were forced by law to leave their homes because of the colour of their skins. Father, forgive us.'

It was profound, and probably the reason why Bonita's haunting question about dying of a broken heart hit me so hard. As a newsman with a cynical inclination that had developed in newsrooms, I couldn't reconcile with the notion. But after speaking to Bonita, I wasn't so sure, and I was prepared to concede that, in the case of District Six at least, someone could have died of a broken heart.

It is a notion Bonita grappled with too. In her 15 years of being exposed to the storied history of District Six, she had heard it over and over. 'People died, people actually lost their minds,' Bonita said in the interview.' I wasn't quite sure what to make of oral history when people say, "My mother died of a broken heart." 'Was this just a melodramatic way of telling a story? What do people actually mean? You get a notice and you collapse and you die. The other thing people would say was, "My father was never the same again."

'People talk about mental illness in a very coded way. I think that was often a reference, because they would talk about their fathers moving to Manenberg. These fathers would get lost and they would eventually find them in this barren wasteland, sitting there where their house used to be. That's a sign of mental illness and never recovering.

'I did those interviews about 15 years ago. My understanding of the way depression and the impact of negative trauma on the human psyche affects the physical body is that you can actually – not immediately – but you can actually die of a broken heart.

'Someone also recounts this story of how this family was in conflict about whether they were going to move or resist. In the midst of this argument the father has a heart attack and dies. Their memory is that their father died because of forced removals. I suppose there were underlying conditions to the health; so I think the forced removals were probably the cherry on top.

'That is what we're able to do with the museum – the human experience. It's very time-consuming and human resource-intensive, but it is an important humanising of the District Six story. There were the minstrels celebrating – rising up from the ashes – but there were also people who never recovered.'

In Bonita's family too, there was a yearning for their lives back in District Six. She wasn't born at the time of the actual declaration and the family was already living in Bonteheuwel before all the homes in District Six were destroyed. But Bonteheuwel was never considered home. Her childhood memories were all about District Six. Her relationship with District Six started as a five-year-old, always in transit from the family home in Bonteheuwel to spend every moment they could in District Six, as the houses started being reduced to rubble, little by little. Some fought until the bitter end. Others accepted their lot as soon as the eviction notices arrived at their door.

'It's been a very interesting journey for me, because I just missed the actual declaration of District Six. In a strange way, there is a whole group of people – and a debate has started in the museum – who question whether Bonteheuwel was really a creation after the declaration of District Six,' said Bonita.[9] Bonteheuwel came about in 1960 and the actual declaration of District Six was in 1966. I think from the Group Areas Act and the Population Registrations Act from the 1950s. People were living in anticipation that resistance was going to fail. A lot of families, like my parents, would normally add on to the house or make a home in the district as the children got married. But they started not doing that. They started moving out of the district.

'My relationship with District Six was that I grew up with a very strange consciousness actually, and I tried to explain this to some people, which I can only intuitively understand. But I can't really explain how I grew up in Bonteheuwel but thought of District Six as home. 'I recall my mom always saying, "We live in Bonteheuwel, but it's not our home." Growing up with that, I didn't particularly question it. When you hear something often enough, you just accept it as a truth until you're like 12 or 13, when you become more philosophical. You then start asking, "Haven't we lived here long enough to make this our home?"

'I don't think that's a unique story. A lot of us grew up in places that didn't feel like home and that you were hankering, like our parents, for something else. I grew up in Bonteheuwel, but all my childhood memories were District Six.

'We were also one of those families who, on Friday, when you came from school, my mother had our bags packed, we were in the bus, getting off in Constitution Street (District Six), where my aunt lived, and Monday morning we were back in Bonteheuwel.

'My childhood formation in terms of holidays and weekends was Sunday School (at St Philip's in Chapel Street), my father playing in the band – so weekends were also spent either in the dance halls, falling asleep on a band member's lap or following the Christmas bands and Malay Choirs.

'My childhood memories are of District Six and sometimes I have to remind myself that, technically, I didn't actually grow up there.'

For others, their memories of District Six were born on the stage and are a romantic idea of what the suburb was all about. Talented young performers like Alistair Izobell, Loukmaan Adams and Emo Adams – all protegés of the Taliep Petersen-David Kramer anthology of musicals – ensured that the memory of District Six was kept alive in song and on stage. There was *District Six – The Musical, Fairyland*, and *Kat and the Kings*, to name a few. *Kat and the Kings* in particular, was a rip-roaring success, as it told the story of a four-part harmony singing group from the 1950s. *Kat and the Kings* is based on the life of Salie Daniels, who grew up in District Six and started a vocal harmony group. He played the narrator of the musical, looking back at his younger self and how the band eventually split up because the suburb was being destroyed. The musical travelled incredibly well all over the world and struck a chord with audiences. Loukmaan Adams won a Laurence Olivier Award and a Tony Award for his performance in *Kat and the Kings* in London's West End and New York's Broadway.

In 2016, David Kramer – this time without his partner, Taliep Petersen, who had been murdered a few years earlier – cast Loukmaan again to star in a brand new musical called *District Six Kanala* (a colloquial word for 'please' in the Cape Malay community). It was especially produced to mark the 50th anniversary of the apartheid government's declaration of District Six as a whites-only area. Loukmaan jumped at the opportunity. District Six was a special place for him, not only because he played so many District Six characters over more than three decades, but also because his father used to regale him and his brother Emo with stories of the area. *District Six Kanala* would be a celebration of all the stage tributes to the area over the years and a chance to educate a new generation about District Six.

'We're celebrating a space; a space that should have been here,' he told me in a Friday Files interview ahead of the opening night of *District Six Kanala*. 'I look at Bo-Kaap because a similar thing could have happened there, and right now it's probably one of the biggest tourist attractions.

'If you look at pictures of District Six, these houses should still have been here. I look at those buildings - and I think, "Wow, imagine these buildings were still here. It would have been one of the most expensive areas in town."

'We're trying to remember that and celebrate that. We don't dwell on the ugliness of how people were removed, but it was where our forefathers lived. The youth need to know where they come from; where their forefathers come from. It's a part of their history. The days when Taliep wrote these songs – it's not just a song, you feel it.

'I don't know if Taliep's spirit is there, but as soon as you sing these songs, it just does something. We also pay tribute to Salie Daniels and perform some of his songs. It's emotional and a lot of people are going to cry. Everything I know about District Six I either got from my parents or people who lived there. Taliep couldn't stop talking about District Six. David knows a lot about it. He had to give us the stories, especially with this younger cast.'

There were two stark truths that Loukmaan mentioned in that interview. The first was that Bo-Kaap could have gone the same way. The other was that District Six would probably have become one of the most expensive areas to buy property in Cape Town.

The irony is that the Bo-Kaap moment happened more than 20 years into our democracy. The creep of gentrification was slowly taking over, with the City of Cape Town aiding and abetting new arrivals in the neighbourhood. There were complaints too about the call to prayers that have been a feature of the Bo-Kaap – which has the oldest mosque in Cape Town – since it became an area for Cape Malay slaves who were predominantly Muslim. Then bottle stores opened. Then a massive Hilton Hotel. And slowly but surely the rich and foreign buyers were making residents of Bo-Kaap offers for their homes that they simply couldn't refuse.

But things came to a head when a developer decided to build a high-rise block of flats in the historic suburb. A group of young people banded together and decided that enough was enough. They were not going to entertain anyone who was going to mess with the rich heritage of their area. They blocked the streets, burnt tyres and caused a general ruckus in the area, which is in the heart of Cape Town's CBD. Increasingly, the older generation started joining the protest. Never before had the community stood together as one like this – even though there were some who sided with the developers.

While there was an ongoing and protracted legal battle in court between the ratepayers' association and the developer over an interdict to stop the development of the high-rise residential building, the residents won the day when the Bo-Kaap was afforded heritage status. It was a victory, because now the City of Cape Town would treat all applications for development in the area with greater circumspection.

As for District Six, it is anyone's guess what is to become of the prime, yet barren land. The Western Cape Government promised to build 10 000 inner city homes, but that figure was suddenly reduced to 2 000 with no explanation given, according to a report by Sune Payne of the *Daily Maverick*. She added that no inner-city houses had been built, despite promises made over more than two decades, except for the few units that were presented to returning residents at the so-called District Six Homecoming in the early 2000s. That now seems more than ever like a PR stunt and a sham. To add insult to injury, the technikon has since extended its footprint further across District Six with accommodation blocks for students. All indications are that gentrification will kill the dream of past District Six residents ever returning in a meaningful way. It's just not realistic, but I do hope that I'm wrong. A few good people, like High Court Judge, Justice Siraj Desai, and up until recently the late activist Dr Anwah Nagia, have fought for the right of the displaced people of District Six to return.

While District Six and Sophiatown in Johannesburg were the prominent stories of the Group Areas Act, there are so many other examples of apartheid spatial planning's evil perfection that live on to this day. During my reporting days, I was always struck by just how effectively the town planners of the day segregated people based on the colour of their skin. Take a drive through the quiet, coastal town of Kleinmond, for example, and you will see apartheid's racial segregation still at play. You'll start driving past the plush homes of retired white couples or those who can afford holiday homes. A few kilometres further on is the main road and the town's CBD, which is the only time you will see people of different races interacting. A few kilometres past this shopping area, you'll find the RDP houses for the coloured community – about 24 square metres in size. Then, even further from the shops and amenities, you'll find the black informal settlement, with even smaller shacks. It's like the New South Africa never reached Kleinmond. And there are replicas of Kleinmond all over the Western Cape.

My family and I spent one New Year's Eve at the Caledon Hotel and Casino. I've never wanted to go back and the Twitter thread that I wrote on 1 January 2018 will tell you why:[10]

'1. The next thread is a story about service delivery – or specifically lack thereof – in the Western Cape town of Caledon.

2. The story starts on New Year's Eve 2017, just after 10pm. The Caledon Hotel and Spa – including the casino – is plunged into darkness. Less than 30 seconds later, the power is restored.

3. The hotel management must be relieved, because they've invited a host of VIP guests to see in the new year.

4. But the staff at the hotel tell a different story this morning. Folks had been looking forward to the New Year's Eve foam party at the local club, BJ's, for weeks now. Imagine the disappointment when the power went down after 10pm and never came back on.

5. But last night wasn't an isolated event for the people of Caledon. While power to the well-heeled spending NYE at the hotel was restored instantly, NYE for the ordinary folk was ruined. No reason or explanation given.

6. The staff are quietly upset this morning while going about their work. They say the power cuts happen regularly and for long periods at a time. But they never read about it in their local paper.

7. So this is how municipalities and Eskom in rural towns escape accountability. No one makes waves, there is no story here, it's not like it happened at the hotel, right?

8. However, it's a powder keg. The anger will simmer into resentment and soon after protest action. We've seen these go violent so many times. And then the symptoms are addressed when there is no real accountability.

9. How many other Caledons exist in SA? Away from the media's glare, where mayors and service providers like Eskom can operate with impunity. This small example drives home the point of how important a robust media is.

10. I leave Caledon today to return to the City of Cape Town, where I can tweet whenever I'm dissatisfied with something. There will always be a response and some action. But what about the people of Caledon? Is this democracy?

My Twitter thread was hardly an incitement to violence, but lo and behold, it took the community an entire year to finally get fed up.

In a report that appeared on the *News24* website in April 2019, reporter Jenni Evans wrote: 'Deputy Police Minister Bongani Mkongi called for calm in Caledon on Friday following the deaths of two people during a protest in the Western Cape town.

'"Today we visited Caledon following the death of two protesters and interacted with the community and its leaders," he said on his Facebook page on Friday.

'"It is alleged that the protesters were shot by police," he said. "During our interaction we reiterated our message conveyed earlier by our National Commissioner (Khehla Sitole) that it is our humble appeal that the community of Caledon remain calm and allow the investigation to take its course."

'On Thursday, two men were killed during a march, over service delivery and housing, from Uitsig and Riemvasmaak to the Theewaterskloof municipal offices.'

Back in Woodstock, where I grew up, and in Salt River, where I went to school and played sport, which is closer to the media,[11] the war of attrition is subtle. It is a gradual wearing down of residents with big offers for their homes. It started with the arrival of the Biscuit Mill – a high-end retail development that quite frankly isn't at all affordable for the people who live in Woodstock and Salt River. Then the entire Albert Road, from my old Essex Street home to the Salt River circle, became hipster heaven. Boutique stores selling refurbished furniture, artisanal food stores and crappy little pretentious art galleries. Poor Mr Narker, the Indian shopkeeper who owned Runwell Superette, which was a fixture on the corner of Essex Street and Albert Road for decades, eventually succumbed and sold up. It is now called The Runwell and no one from the area eats there.

I drive through my old neighbourhood of Woodstock and the characters who sold drugs some 20 years after I left are still there. Gentrification, this sophisticated way of bullying people out of their neighbourhoods in a much less brutal way than the authorities dealt with folk in District Six, hasn't exactly cured the social ills. There's prosperity, yes, but none of it is meant for the people from the area.

One business owner, Reaaz Ahmed, who I am proud to call a friend and whose family started Good Hope Butchery at the Salt River Circle, is like the indomitable Gauls of the Asterix and Obelix comic books, who the Romans just can't get a handle on. The business is now called Good Hope Meat Hyper and it is in the same location, but its premises have grown substantially in size. Reaaz says not a week goes by when some character doesn't come into the store to offer him and his family a ridiculous sum of money for the property. Reaaz sends them packing. Like his father before him, it was decades ago when he first started the butcher shop. Reaaz is too invested in the community to ever sell out. He supports other local businesses and the various community football clubs, and is always ready to give back.

The problem is, there are not enough people like Reaaz who will stand firm and defy the attempt to rob Woodstock and Salt River of its identity. And as the demand for inner city housing continues to rise and greedy developers with no care for the wellbeing of the people cash in, so entire communities will be stripped of their character and DNA.

Welcome to Cape Town!

23 March 2005. The infamous Jesus Lives in My Toilet front page. ©*Independent Media*

24 March 2005. A follow up by the *Daily Voice* to the infamous Jesus Lives in My Toilet front page. ©*Independent Media*

30 July 2011. Archbishop Thabo Makgoba, Anglican Archbishop of Cape Town, leads a delegation from the Western Cape Religious Leaders' Forum (WCRLF) with Imam Rashid Omar, to a number of informal settlements in Khayelitsha to stand in solidarity with people without adequate sanitation. ©*ANA Pictures*

10 April 2016. Then *Cape Argus* editor Gasant Abarder pours over the front page lead story copy written by homeless columnist Danny Oosthuizen ahead of the following day's historic edition of the newspaper to launch The Dignity Project. ©*Ross Jansen/African News Agency*

11 April 2016. The *Cape Argus* enters uncharted terrain as Danny Oosthuizen, a homeless man, writes the front page lead of the newspaper. The piece launched a memorable editorial collaboration between the newspaper and homeless people in Cape Town called The Dignity Project. ©*Independent Media*

9 November 2019. Danny Oosthuizen, the homeless man who wrote a column for the *Cape Argus* and helped thaw relations between authorities and the homeless of Cape Town with the Dignity Project, celebrating his last birthday at a surprise party thrown by the newspaper. Former editor Gasant Abarder was one of the guests. ©*Gasant Abarder*

9 November 2019. Danny Oosthuizen admires the cake supplied by the *Cape Argus* for his surprise 50th birthday party. ©*Ayanda Ndamane/African News Agency*

23 September 2013. Rashied Staggie, former co-leader of the Hard Livings gang, visits London Road in Salt River where his twin brother Rashaad was shot and killed after a march to his home. Rashied would be murdered in the same road outside his house in December 2019. ©*African News Agency*

Given a chance to prove himself

Friday Files

By Gasant Abarder

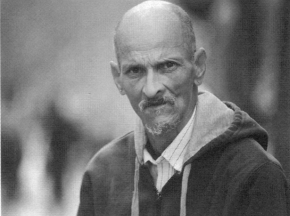

CHANGED MAN: Magadien Wentzel is an ex-28s gang member and the subject of the book, *The Number*, by Jonny Steinberg.   Picture: DAVID RITCHIE

MAGADIEN WENTZEL has a spring in his step and a smile on his face. It's a far cry from the man I featured in the Friday Files about 18 months ago. Then he was ready to give up and was even contemplating going back to prison.

In July 2016, Magadien had been out of prison for 12 years and on the straight and narrow for 16.

But the former senior-ranking member of the 28s prison gang, who was the central focus of Jonny Steinberg's book, *The Number*, was battling to find his place in society after turning his back on the gang.

But mostly, Magadien was seeking redemption for his wrongs.

When we spoke Magadien, 56, kept repeating that he wanted an opportunity to prove his worth.

Now it is evident that Magadien has found his purpose.

His confidence is back and, as we make our way to Mariam's Kitchen for breakfast, Magadien, wearing a red T-shirt with a large print of the crest of his beloved Manchester United, starts bickering with Liverpool fans.

It's all friendly banter though and I can't help thinking how just 18 months ago he may have withdrawn or could have reacted very differently.

It all started changing for Magadien shortly after that first Friday Files profile, when I connected him with the former University of Western Cape restoration chairperson, Brian Williams.

Brian was putting together a peace ambassador programme to intervene with youth at risk of gangs and drugs in the Kensington and Factreton area. It didn't take much persuasion on my part for Brian to include Magadien in the programme as one of the trainee peace ambassadors.

It was a turning point for Magadien. His life experiences proved invaluable to the programme and his peers.

However, when he graduated from the programme in October last year, he would make a decision that would change the course of his life.

"When you introduced me to Brian Williams, I was very sceptical. People make promises and then they disappoint me. But I thought, let me listen to what this guy has to say.

"He actually showed me quite the opposite. He kept his word and invited me to the peace-building training.

"At the end of the training each of us had to select a project. I didn't know what to do.

"Most of the people were from the Factreton and Kensington area. I was one of the only people in the group from outside the area. I had to come up with a project that would benefit society and the people.

"I thought long and hard and then got a call from a woman from Kinfisa Social Solutions in Joburg. She told me she had a colleague in Cape Town, Jesse Laitinen. I had a meeting with them and agreed to check it out because I had nothing to lose by volunteering my services.

"I started facilitating some workshops for the homeless like peace building, anger management and restoring dignity. I was the new guy on the block and the

> ## WHEN YOU INTRODUCED ME TO BRIAN WILLIAMS, I WAS VERY SCEPTICAL. PEOPLE MAKE PROMISES AND THEN THEY DISAPPOINT ME. BUT I THOUGHT LET ME LISTEN TO WHAT THIS GUY HAS TO SAY.

guy that was in charge felt a bit threatened because he thought I might come and take over his space.

"We got a contract from the City of Cape Town and were able to employ some people. I was asked to be a supervisor and thought it couldn't be that hard to supervise homeless people. My style differed from other supervisors: I would talk to them, didn't rush or threaten them and I listened to their stories to see where I could help.

"I thought I should set the stage for them so that they could perform. I called in a few guests to speak to the group to expose them to people from all walks of life."

It was during one of these sessions, with me as Magadien's invited guest as the then-Cape Argus editor, that The Dignity Project was born.

Magadien was instrumental in its conception.

He opened my eyes to the possibility of linking homeless people's skills with jobs and improving their lot and roles in society.

I spoke to the group of homeless people for a few minutes before being completely engrossed in their stories.

While we were writing about The Dignity Project in the Cape Argus, Magadien was hard at work creating a garden off Roeland Street on what was nothing more than a vacant lot with a gravel surface.

Today it's a vibrant food garden that employs the homeless. The fresh produce finds its way to the plates of patrons of leading restaurants and eateries in the Cape Town CBD.

"I brought you in and out of that The Dignity Project was born. From there the project really grew because now people saw the homeless in a different light.

"They saw that people cared and the project went from strength to strength.

"That was one of the things that I wanted to turn around: why must people beg? It's not dignified to beg and it's not a nice thing. It's not a nice thing for people to have no shoes and no clothes. I know how that feels.

"When I was there... when I was released as a changed man, society turned its back on me. There were a few individuals who I could call on and say I need this or that – but not for myself, for the projects I was involved in."

Last week Magadien hosted a Christmas party for poor children with donations from friends and acquaintances he has met over the years. In the more than a decade I have known him he has never asked for anything for himself, but always for things that would help young people at risk.

During that first interview Magadien's health wasn't great. He had just recovered from a serious bout of pneumonia and looked haggard and frail. Today he looks younger and as if several burdens have

been lifted from his shoulders.

Relations with his family have improved too. Magadien beams with pride when he talks about his seven grandchildren, although he worries about the eldest who is at risk of being drawn into a gang.

"It's my approach to life. I don't believe in governmental laws, I hate it. I hate any law except the universal law. Universal law says what is up, most come down. If you put bad in you get bad out. If you put good in, you get good out.

"It has nothing to do with religion, it is just life. What I'm putting in with my grandchildren, I am seeing the returns. It's not about buying expensive presents but it's about making time for them.

"What makes me feel better is that when you are happy with what you are doing and you are doing positive things, then you become more positive. I wasn't in distress and I wasn't angry. As a matter of fact, I was happy."

But there's more positivity on the horizon for Magadien in 2017. Next year, a film based on his life and the book, *The Number*, is due to be released on circuit. Magadien spent a month in Durban as an on-set adviser a few weeks ago at the behest of award-winning director Khalo Matabane.

"When Khalo came to me for the first time, what must I remember by then he was the third guy who said they wanted to make a film about me. The other two... I don't know where they disappeared to but they disappeared.

"When Khalo came to me I listened and my exact words to him were, 'Okay, I'll see if it materialises'. It took him six years and I only believed that it was happening when I got the message from him that I was booked on a flight to Durban where they wanted me to assist and advise on set.

"Only then I knew the film was going to become a reality. It's about my life and that's why I was there to advise and see

that everything is on point.

"You must remember that the condition to agreeing to this film is not about sensationalism or my backe. My interest in making this movie and being part of it is that it must be an education tool.

"My job is to see that this film is used to build the community. It's one of my requests. Even if it has an age restriction, they must cut out the hardcore scenes to make it acceptable for schools.

"Life is still a challenge for Magadien but he is looking forward and not back.

When he turned his back on the gang, he signed his own death sentence because it was an act that was punishable by death.

But 18 months ago, Magadien was more worried about dying of boredom.

There is no danger of that now after he has tasted the rewards of devoting his life to the service of others.

The past war has given him the self-belief that he can make a difference, but more importantly for his own sense of self-worth, he has realised that society needs him.

"My belief is that you can only release yourself from poverty if you give your children the opportunity to become successful. That is the key that will take you out of that Aobbie or crowded braces.

"One thing that I can honestly say is that 2016 was the best year of my life. For the first time, for one year, I could do good for a whole year – even if society didn't notice.

"One thing that I, Magadien, am proud of is that for a year I could dedicate my life in the service of the homeless and see how they grow, see how some of them change their years, see how some of them move back to their families, and see how some of them – through my intervention – could reconcile with society. There are no words to comprehend how I feel. I proved yet again to society that I could make a difference if given the opportunity to engage."

December 2016. Author Gasant Abarder forged a close bond with Magadien Wentzel. The former prison gang leader turned his life around – but not after battling for more than a decade for a chance at redemption as, time and time again, society turned its back on him. ©*Independent Media*

Date Unknown. Celeste and Morné Nurse spent 17 years looking for Zephany Nurse and never gave up hope. After Zephany's 17th birthday their dream of finding their daughter came true. But it was anything but a happy ending. ©*African News Agency*

Date unknown. Zephany Nurse doing a radio interview at *CapeTalk 567* at the time of the launch of her book following a dramatic and drawn out court case involving the woman she thought was her biological mother but turned out to be her kidnapper. ©*African News Agency*

Date Unknown. Matthew Ohlsson disappeared from in front of his family's Mitchells Plain home under mysterious circumstances. More than 30 years later he was never seen or heard from again. © *Supplied/African News Agency*

1994. Norman Afzal Simons, the 'Station Strangler', suspected of being a notorious serial killer, arrives in police custody at the Kuils River Magistrate's Court on a charge related to the murder of Elroy van Rooyen, whose body was found in a shallow grave in nearby Melton Rose. © *Leon Muller/African News Agency*

23 September 2019. Prince Harry and Meghan Markle are greeted by Bonita Bennett, the Director of District Six Museum, who lead them on a tour of the exhibitions at the museum. ©*Bertram Malgas/African News Agency*

4 August 2020. The historic Bo-Kaap suburb in the heart of the Cape Town CBD has been the scene of pitched battles between residents and law enforcement officers over the threat of urban creep. The area has since been declared a heritage site, which gives it some measure of preservation against gentrification. ©*African News Agency*

20 November 2018. The residents of Bo-Kaap are up in arms and protest against recent developments in the area. The residents made a human chain to block out a crane trying to enter the neighbourhood. ©*Zukiswa Minyi/African News Agency*

22 October 2015. Then editor of the *Cape Argus*, Gasant Abarder (centre), listens attentively as the student co-editors brief him in the news conference boardroom about their special edition the following day. ©*Tracey Adams*

22 October 2015. Two student co-editors of the historic #FeesMustFall special edition of the *Cape Argus* in the newsroom give direction for the layout of their special edition pages. Photo: Tracey Adams/African News Agency. ©*African News Agency*

FRIDAY OCTOBER 23 2015   www.capeargus.co.za

Cape Argus

R7.00
Country R7.00

SPECIAL EDITION LATE FINAL

#ShutItDown

Students call for decolonisation of education, end to outsourcing

Apartheid's Gatherings Act: pasop, black child

Busisiwe Nxumalo
STUDENT PROTESTER

THE DECISION had already been made by the student worker alliance at UCT to protest against fee increases and outsourcing days before the public announcement of a national shutdown of all higher education institutions as a result of ongoing protests.

The alliance resolved to march on Parliament, apart from other affiliates and political parties and organisations who sought to gain political mileage from the protests.

Unarmed activists filled buses from UCT, singing as they made their way to Parliament to join their CPUT and UWC comrades.

On De Waal Drive, our bus was met by police, blocking access to Roeland and Plein streets. Other vehicles were allowed to proceed. Police ordered the bus to turn around and "go back to where it came from".

"Why can't we go through?" students and workers asked in confusion.

The police were waiting outside the bus, armed with stun grenades and tear gas.

As the protesters attempted to disembark, police aggressively blocked people from exiting. Tempers boiled over, with police shouting and becoming physical with protesters.

Undeterred, they managed to disembark and joined fellow comrades on the streets who had also received the same treatment from the police.

Before the group could continue their march in the heat, police announced: "You are not allowed to gather in groups of more than five." The protesters drew together, fearing arrest in the face of multiple police threats.

One of the people in the group was pulled from the crowd and bundled into the back of an awaiting police van.

"What have I done, please let me go," he said.

"Release our comrade, he has done nothing wrong," the crowd shouted in frustration. Police responded by saying: "This is an illegal gathering. You are not allowed to gather in groups of more than five."

A black woman then shouted: "This is not apartheid?"

The comrade was released after continuous demands from protesters. The alliance then peacefully resumed their journey.

They eventually reached Parliament to join fellow protesters from CPUT and UWC. The protesters continued to sing, dance and chant "fees must fall" and "end outsourcing". These strategies were employed by the crowd with the intention of rousing Minister of Higher Education, Dr Blade Nzimande, to leave Parliament and address their demands. Hours went by in the boiling sun with no reply coming from the halls of Parliament.

Unarmed protesters, holding their hands above their heads, only entered Parliament's grounds when police opened the gates.

The police immediately started violently pushing the crowd backward.

A small group slipped past the police cordon and sat in front of the stairs leading up to the National Assembly, chanting: "We want Blade!"

Immediately after that, the police, accompanied by the riot unit and six snipers, arrived to deal with protesters. The protesters sat down to show their intentions were peaceful.

Police then opened fire on the crowd. Stun grenades and tear gas were thrown. Several protesters were also physically assaulted. The protesters were screaming, crying and running away in fear for their lives. In the mist of the pink smoke, you could barely make out a sign that read "1976?".

When the smoke eventually cleared, the crowd regrouped with their hands in the air and sung the national anthem to show that they were still protesting peacefully.

The police again opened fire. After the tear gas smoke cleared, it was evident that there were wounded activists who needed immediate medical care.

"Look, the skin has peeled off on the leg," a protester wailed in between sobs.

A number of students were arrested throughout the week, and one who was arrested on Wednesday, was released yesterday morning before being rearrested in the afternoon.

POLICE BRUTALITY: The ghosts of 1976 haunt students of 2015.   PICTURE: IMRAAN CHRISTIAN

Simon Rakei
STUDENT PROTESTER

LET'S be clear, the legal system was never designed with the intention of protecting the rights of all who live in the land. In fact, it was specifically tailored to protect and preserve the interests of whites and white capital.

Apartheid was permissible by law. Let it be understood that the law never was and will possibly never be a sufficient indicator (perceptor) of what is morally acceptable, of what is right and wrong.

At the end of the apartheid government in 1993, the Gatherings Act was "reformed": gathering was defined as "a march, picket or parade" and not just a group of people in a public space.

Further, the number of people constituting a "group" was revised to 16 or more people, and such gatherings would need a 48-hour notice before they could happen.

Such progress – transformation.

Our, October 19, 2015: 23 students, on university property at UCT, were arrested and charged with contravening the Gatherings Act.

The students were arrested from three different university entrances.

Each entrance had no more than 12 protesters at each location. It is almost appalling that a state which has a black president, government, and police, can still be anti-black in how it defines the value of black lives.

When the police can watch a white student drive a car and ram over two black students without lifting a finger, and yet form a shield around said white student's car when the mob of angry black "savages" start confronting him, it is yet another insightful moment to see the failures of reforms and transformation, and a clear indicator to heed the clarion call for decolonisation.

We must understand that decolonisation is a violent process.

And it is only violent because it challenges the power structure at its very core, and that naturally elicits an unrelenting survival instinct to preserve and maintain institutional power.

Whiteness will not simply abdicate and die – like any living organism, the threat of death will inevitably result in an instinctual response to preserve the self.

It is in this vein we say decolonisation is a violent process.

But it is necessary, because that is the only way we can ever have meaningful change.

In a world which was never made for black people, we can't still be accommodated in this hostile environment which never wanted us.

We must claim those spaces as our own. That is decolonisation.

To that effect, the logical conclusion is a call for the fall of the Gatherings Act.

Clearly, student activism can no longer be "accommodated" under old apartheid laws limiting the ability and right to freedom of expression and assembly.

Student Protester Glossary of Terms

● **Decolonisation** is the removal of all unjust systems, such as patriarchy, racism and capitalism in society and the restructuring of society to reflect African systems.

● **Black:** All racially oppressed people of colour. This political identity goes against the divisive racial categories that were formed during apartheid, such as Indian, Coloured and African. "Black", as a political identity, unites all people of colour who have been socially, politically and economically oppressed.

● **Violence** is an experience of structural oppression. This experience can translate into physical violence, emotional and psychological violence through violent words,

institutional processes, actions and behaviour that are directed at black people in order to dehumanise them. A reaction to this violence is not violence itself, but a defence against dehumanisation.

● **Black pain** is the dehumanisation of black people, which is a daily struggle that comes from the violence that exists in systems that privilege whiteness or is institutionally racist.

● **Whiteness** is a system that privileges white people at the expense of black people. It is present in all institutions in South African society and it is assumed to be the standard of how things should be, but it is inherently racist.

● **Patriarchy** is an unjust political-social system that insists that males are inherently dominant and superior. Everyone else is deemed weak – especially females.

● **LGBTQIA + and gender non-conforming people.** This system privileges men and oppresses everyone that does not conform to the gender roles that society expects. LGBTQIA + – for lesbian, gay, bisexual, transgender/transsexual, intersex, queer and asexual people.

● **White privilege** is a set of advantages or access to certain benefits that have been exclusively developed for white people. White people have white privilege because a system of whiteness is present in South Africa and across the globe, which means that society is structured around white people and their culture.

● **Black Feminism** is a consciousness highlighting black women's experiences in society, which often go unnoticed because black women face alienation based on race, gender and other social factors. This leads to an experience where black women can speak and write about, and from which knowledge can be created.

23 June 2017. Ashley Kriel's sister, Michel Assure, with MK Veterans at a memorial held at the Hazendal house where Ashley Kriel was killed. © *African News Agency*

15 March 2016. Ashley Kriel's sisters, Michel Assure (right) and Melanie Adams (left), pose with a T-shirt bearing his image. Ashley Kriel was shot at a house in Hazendal, Athlone, in 1987. © *David Ritchie/African News Agency.*

3 May 2018. Gasant Abarder with journalist Lukhanyo Calata at the launch of his book, *My Father Died For This*, at the Cape Town library. The book is an investigation by Calata and his wife Abigail Calata into the murders of the Cradock Four – of which Lukhanyo's father Fort Calata was a member. ©*Gasant Abarder*

2018. Lukhanyo Calata was reinstated by the SABC in July 2016 after a legal battle. He has since left the SABC and currently works as programme editor for *e.tv news* and *e.tv sport*. © *Gasant Abarder*

7 January 2020. South African women's football coach Desiree Ellis receives the women's coach of the year award. © *Amr Abdallah Dalsh/Reuters-African News Agency*

19 December 2018. Author Gasant Abarder and Banyana Banyana coach Desiree Ellis at the Cape Town Blitz vs Jozi Stars final match of the Mzansi Super League at Newlands Cricket Ground. © *Gasant Abarder*

Date Unknown. A young Armien Levy took the Cape motorsport scene by storm and later became a multiple champion at Killarney race track. He was the first person of colour to become a champion at Killarney when motorsport was a largely white sport. ©*African News Agency*

19 December 2018. Cape Flats racing legend Armien Levy shares a light-hearted moment with author Gasant Abarder about his driving skills. His daughter Fuzlin Hassen, pictured in the back seat, also caught the bug and had a brief spell racing at Killarney from 1987 to 1989. ©*Gasant Abarder*

2000. A young Gasant Abarder interviews
Archbishop Emeritus Desmond Tutu in
Masiphumelele during a visit to the Desmond
and Leah Tutu Clinic. The clinic began
providing HIV care to Masiphumelele residents
in 1999 and is still situated in the community.
©Benny Gool/Oryx Media Productions

19 August 2015. Then *Cape Argus* editor Gasant
Abarder with Ahmed Kathrada and Eddie Nair
for a *Friday Files* interview ahead of Kathrada
receiving the freedom of the City of Cape Town
award. ©*Cindy Waxa/African News Agency*

September 2010. Then South African National
Editors' Forum (SANEF) Deputy Chairperson,
Gasant Abarder, leads a march of journalists
and media workers to parliament. The march
was against the proposed Protection of State
Information Bill, dubbed the Secrecy Bill.
©*African News Agency*

Date unknown. International award-winning performer, writer and director Ameera Conrad was among a group of students involved in the #FeesMustFall movement who co-edited an edition of of the *Cape Argus* about the student protests. ©*ANA Pictures*

6 #FeesMustFall special edition

'Sacked in the morning! You're getting sacked in the morning! Sacked in the moooooooorning…' (Sung to the tune of *Guantanamera*.) It's a chant that British football fans sing to their opposition rivals when that team's manager is under pressure after a bad run of form.

Why did I have this earworm in my head while standing at Lower Campus at the University of Cape Town on a hot day in October 2015 during a student rally? Because as I stood there, a man in his late 30s in a suit sticking out like a sore thumb, I knew that what I was about to attempt had a good chance of getting me fired. Or it could make history. The stakes were high.

Earlier that morning I had been on my way to the office and was catching up on my Twitter feed while waiting for the traffic light to turn green. It's an awful habit and my kids have drawn pictures of me doing this. Then my eye fell on a tweet from Gus Silber, an author and media trainer who is akin to royalty in the Twittersphere. Gus is one of the nicest guys you'll meet on this often toxic social media platform. But he was also extremely astute as a social commentator.

Gus had tweeted a challenge to newspaper editors to hand over the editing of their newspapers to students involved in the #Fees-MustFall campaign for a day. Without thinking, I replied that as editor of the *Cape Argus*, I accepted the challenge and I would do just that – hand over control of the editorial pages to students fighting to get the government to scrap university tuition fees.

My reply to Gus went viral before I even arrived at the office – even though I had tweeted just a few kilometres away from the basement parking lot. Gus was excited. People started noticing. They were impressed. I realised the enormity of what I had undertaken to do with the next edition of the *Cape Argus*. Now there were hundreds of retweets and likes. Minutes later, I was trending on Twitter in Joburg; then in Cape Town. It was the point of no return.

Walking up from the basement to the ground floor of Newspaper House I started to hurry. It was 10am. How the hell was I going to deliver this? I waited for the lift, pressing the button dozens of times to get it to the ground floor and it felt like an hour had passed. Screw that, I'm taking the stairs to the newsroom on the fourth floor. I was panting heavily but was able to squeeze in a breathless good morning before asking, 'Where's Lance?'

Luckily, Lance Witten was already sitting at his desk.

'What's wrong?' he asked me. I imagined my anxiety had made me look as green as an alien.

'Have you seen the challenge I accepted on Twitter?', I asked before passing him my phone so he could read the tweet.

He read it and put on his thinking face. Then his face lit up before he exclaimed with a smile, 'Oh shit! This is brilliant.'

But how? How would we get a group of students to agree to edit an edition of the *Cape Argus*? Where would we find them? Would they even be receptive to the idea, since they'd been complaining that the mainstream media only quoted official sources and didn't give the students an opportunity to tell their side of the story?

Lance sprang into action and we put out a call to action from the *Cape Argus* official Twitter account, calling on students to edit the next day's paper. While everyone loved the idea, not one student put a hand up to indicate they would like to have a crack at what I was offering.

Then I got a WhatsApp that would determine how the next news day would turn out for me. It was Beauregard Tromp, the deputy editor of the Mail & Guardian. We had studied together at journalism school and we were good mates. He was calling to congratulate me on a fine idea. Then I shared with him how we were battling to round up a group of students to participate.

When I explained my challenge, Beauregard's words to me were simple, yet they made so much sense that I was almost taken aback by his presence of mind and clarity. 'Go there and humble yourself. You can't do something like this and expect the students to come to you. You need to go to the campuses and appeal to students to get involved,' he said.

And that was that. 'Let's go get some students!' I told Lance.

The clock was ticking and time was against us. It was just after 11am and we would miss the morning news conference. No one else in the newsroom knew what we were about to do. I told my personal assistant, Lyntina Aimes, that the team must go ahead with the conference in my absence and I would explain everything when I got back. The reason I wanted the team to prepare an alternative plan for the next day's paper was because I wanted a contingency in case my plan went belly-up.

We raced out of the basement parking lot in my car. 'The University of Cape Town's Hiddingh Campus?,' I asked Lance. Then I answered my own question, 'Nah – too arty.'

UCT's main campus was the closest option for us to find our student editors for tomorrow's edition. As we approached UCT, we first tried Upper Campus, but it was a scene of … well, it may as well have been of tumbleweeds across a desolate plain. A lone student told us the students were gathering at Lower Campus, so that's where we headed. Hundreds of students had gathered around a massive tree that was generous with its shade.

It was a few days after students had shut down campuses across the country. They had marched to parliament, demanding free university tuition and an end to outsourcing certain services, among other demands. Things turned nasty quickly when police moved against the students and a few were arrested and hurt in the scuffles.

Now, just days later, in the middle of this gathering, stood the diminutive figure of a young woman delivering a stirring poem she had written. It seemed to have struck a chord with her comrades, because as soon as she had finished reading the poem there were several calls of 'Amandla!'

Here was a potential leader, I thought. I sent in my wingman, Mr Witten – who has a very charming disposition in difficult situations like these – to first approach young Ameera Conrad. A few minutes later we had rounded up five students who had agreed that they would take us up on the offer to edit the next day's edition of the *Cape Argus*.

As we drove back to the office, we chit-chatted with Ameera and her fellow students who were crammed into the back of my sedan. I could sense that they were suspicious of us and I was that awkward old dude again – trying too hard, like I did with Danny Oosthuizen.

But we did quickly gauge from them on the trip back to the newsroom that the #FeesMustFall movement didn't have a hierarchy. There were no leaders, so there was no one to consult about doing what these students were about to do. This was going to be a problem, I thought.

At the best of times, a newspaper cannot be run as a democracy. Yes, editors must listen. Sometimes you get the best editorial ideas from the cleaner. But ultimately, after considering all the options, you have to be decisive as an editor, as the buck stops with you. You're going to carry the can. But if there were no leaders among these students, who was going to make the final decisions? Newspapers are run on deadlines. Without them, everything else falls apart.

It was just after noon. I called the staff into the conference room and invited the group of students inside. They would be joined by a few more students later that day. At that moment though, I could see the horror in my colleagues' eyes at what I had to say next. Especially, my dear former colleague Robyn Leary. Robyn was my assistant editor, a fine production editor and often the handbrake to some of my crazier ideas. But this time she didn't protest and listened intently instead.

The students would be given exactly half of the news pages – five out of the 10 news pages for tomorrow's edition. In addition, the leader article – the one usually reserved for the editor to write – and the opinion page were reserved for the students as well. I would not interfere with any of the pages, except to outline the parameters of what was possible in terms of deadline, and to help them with the production of the pages. The headlines, copy, captions and picture selection would be left entirely up to them. I had given the students until about 1.30pm to tell me their plan. At 2pm, the regular editorial meeting would commence and the students would be part of that as well.

My team shuffled nervously back to their desks to work on the rest of the paper. Now I had serious doubts. I'd worked in newsrooms for almost two decades by then, and I knew how difficult it was to fill five pages with quality editorial with a short copy deadline of 6pm.

So I left the co-editors of the next day's edition of the *Cape Argus* to plot their edition in the conference room: Ameera Conrad, Dela Gwala, Leila Khan, Brian Kamanzi, Mbali Matandela, Amanda Xulu, Busisiwe Nxumalo and Simon Rakei. To be honest, I didn't think these young people would pull it off.

I shuffled nervously back into the conference room to let them know I had ordered pizza and some drinks for them while they plotted ahead. What I really wanted was to get a handle on whether they were making progress. But I left them to it.

I sat nervously at the newsdesk with my feet up so as not to show my growing panic. It was usually where I located myself at the business end of the day. My cellphone rang and it was Karima Brown, our group editorial executive director. Some of my other editor colleagues were intimidated by Karima. She was strong but fair and didn't suffer fools. Her job was to ensure the group's titles stuck to their core readership and audience in a focused way, and to help us strategise to grow the titles.

I remember her asking what was going on and that she had heard that students were co-editing the next day's paper. To her credit, Karima listened carefully. The reason I had a rapport with Karima was because I came from the same neighbourhood and we had both attended Salt River High – albeit during different eras. Karima was tough and didn't mince her words. But I had grown up alongside many Karimas and knew that their tough talking, with the odd expletive included, wasn't to be confused with their sensitive nature. And being the professional journalist Karima was, she immediately recognised the significance of what the *Cape Argus* was about to do.

'It sounds brilliant, Gasant. I can't wait to see it tomorrow."

And that was that. Karima had complete faith that I knew exactly what I was doing (even though I wasn't entirely sure!) and loved the principle of our giving the voiceless a voice. Maybe I'd still have a job the next day.

Too quickly for my liking, 1.30pm rolled around. It was time for the moment of truth. The students told me their plan and it blew me away. The clarity of thought, and the understanding of how newspapers worked and what they wanted to say, was impressive. While there wasn't a leader, I was particularly impressed by Brian Kamanzi, who had been elected to speak on behalf of the student co-editors. What the students had lined up, as I would later tweet, was not a mommy's *Cape Argus*. I warned our readers that they should be prepared to be offended.

At 2pm, I was happy to share the news conference with my student co-editors. By then my team had just about wrapped up the rest of the news pages. We were praying there wouldn't be a big, breaking news story to throw a spanner in the works, and fortunately there wasn't. Then I sat back as the student co-editors explained their plan. There was doubt in the room that they could pull it off; but Brian Kamanzi gave me a strange sense of calm and I was starting to believe.

We located the students at workstations and they filed their stories via their personal Gmail accounts. The copy started streaming in. In fact, they beat the copy deadline easily, with some excellent pieces being filed. The content hit all the right notes. This was their protest and they were determined to use the pages of the *Cape Argus* to tell the world their story.

I asked our Chief Sub, Colin Appolis, if the copy was okay. He had a smile on his face, for once, and said the copy was some of the cleanest he had seen in a while. There were so few errors that when I read through the copy myself I battled to find even the smallest spelling or grammatical error.

The students had found one of their peers who was documenting the protest to send through a selection of pictures. We were now gathered around Colin's workstation and I was helping them with headlines for their pieces – being very careful not to be prescriptive, of course.

The main image (by Imraan Christian) on the front page was well chosen. It was a picture of scores of students gathered outside Parliament just before all hell broke loose. In the middle of the image was a young lady – the only one facing the camera. (Her peers were chatting away and oblivious to the camera.) She was holding aloft a poster that read, simply: '1976?'

Busisiwe Nxumalo wrote a first-person account for the lead story on the front page of what happened leading up to the student protest and the aftermath. The headline read, '#ShutItDown', with the subhead reading: 'Students call for decolonisation of education, end to outsourcing'.

The sidebar accompanying the lead story was written by Simon Rakei. In it, Simon explained how the police had used apartheid's illegal gatherings act to move against the students. A glossary for the less 'woke' rounded off the page, providing definitions and explanations for terms such as decolonisation, blackness, violence, black pain, whiteness, patriarchy, LGBTQIA+, gender conforming people, white privilege and black feminism.

Reading through the proofs of their five news pages was an education for me. The older generation, including the author of this book, were constantly accusing young people of apathy, being disengaged and even of being lazy. But reading the copy, they were anything but.

The #FeesMustFall movement, with the #RhodesMustFall movement as its forerunner, had awoken a sleeping giant. The students were honouring the activism of the students of the 1970s and 1980s. But this time it wasn't directed at an illegitimate government that oppressed black people with apartheid. This time the students were reminding the older generation about activism and holding power to account – even when it was a democratically elected government that they were protesting against.

Earlier in the year, the #RhodesMustFall protests saw activism by students that took many by surprise. It started with a lone student throwing faeces at the UCT statue of Cecil John Rhodes, a historical figure identified as the coloniser-in-chief. The protests then spiraled until the university management was forced to take a decision to have the Rhodes statue removed. The students had won the battle, but the war had just begun.

Next up, was the fight for free tuition, an end to outsourcing of labour at universities and the decolonisation of higher education institutions. The movement, later dubbed #FeesMustFall, spread like wildfire across all South African campuses, and ultimately culminated in a massive standoff between police and students on the lawns of the Union Buildings.

Outgoing president Jacob Zuma's parting shot as he was about to exit from the Presidency was to announce that tuition would be free for first year students in a phased-in approach towards fee-free tertiary education, leaving the new president, Cyril Ramaphosa, and his administration to deal with a promise they're still battling to meet.

But the pages of the *Cape Argus* came to life with so much more. Throughout, the copy was a social commentary, a snapshot if you like, about the inequality of South African life. They were asking the hard questions. Where was the promise of the Freedom Charter that proclaimed that the doors of learning shall be open? They delved into how #FeesMustFall affected us all, from UCT to Khayelitsha. Why was the cost of basic foodstuff like bread and milk out of reach of millions of South Africans?

Of course, earlier in the year, the students didn't endear themselves to the establishment when they set art alight and started destroying property on the campuses.

The student co-editors provided an accompanying image of themselves covering their faces with posters that read #FeesMustFall and #EndOutsourcing, and wrote the following in their message to the readers:

'The *Cape Argus* invited student co-editors to edit this edition of the newspaper.

'What you read from page 1 to page 5, the leader article and the op-ed piece, was written, commissioned and edited by the students involved in the #FeesMustFall protest.

'The student co-editors had carte blanche on news selection for these pages, deciding on the news hierarchy. The student co-editors had the final say on pictures, headlines, captions and subheads, and had the final eye before pages were signed off.

'In a response to the *Cape Argus*, who made the offer to lend its resources to the voices of student protesters, the student co-editors gathered in the newsroom and made an effort to provide context by pooling articles and perspectives from various contexts to help start what is clearly going to be a long national conversation.

'The student co-editors collectively call into scrutiny the handling of the student protests by the media thus far and we urge the relevant parties to reach out to young people on the ground with the intention of listening, instead of recreating harmful ill-disguised colonial stereotypes of masses of young black people who are painted as violent and unthinking, but are in reality making a resolute stand for justice.

– Student co-editors: Ameera Conrad, Dela Gwala, Leila Khan, Brian Kamanzi, Mbali Matandela, Amanda Xulu, Busisiwe Nxumalo, Simon Rakei.'

The leader editorial article, the one that the editor usually uses to opine on issues of the day, was a no-holds-barred slap in the face by Ameera Conrad.

She wrote under the headline: 'The kids are not OK

'It's difficult to explain why young people are so angry. Let's be honest here, we're all angry and we all hate everything and that's what seems to define our generation, but every time someone older than 30 tries to adult-splain what it means to be young it feels like bashing your head against a wall.

'It's not like there aren't issues. People seem to think that the second apartheid ended, this magic TRC wand was waved and suddenly all of our problems were gone.

'This is a lie. This is the biggest lie that our parents ever fed us. This is the biggest lie that our government ever fed us.

'Black people are stuck. And after 21 years of swimming, we're finally coming up to breathe, but we're finding that we can't, because so-called "adults" keep trying to cover our mouths.

'People keep trying to shove this idea of a peaceful and unified Rainbow Nation down our throats with their Bokke Friday and their #ProteaFire, but our country is on fire, and until recently the "adults" haven't noticed.

'The kids are not okay. We've had enough of your Rainbow-tinted Ray-Bans, Mom and Dad.

'Our predecessors have dug our grave and this government has started shovelling sand onto us. But we're climbing out. And you can't stop us.

'It starts with statues. It starts with the symbols that oppress us by their very existence. It ends... Well, who knows how it'll end? This country is fooled by the belief that we're all equal because Mandela said we would be, but we're not.

'This country has vomited apartheid and the youth are sick of the bile burning our throats. We're done being polite and sitting side by side with those who systematically oppress us – we want true freedom, and not the kind Pharrell Williams profits from on iTunes.

'So, ja okay, take your car-flag, but take it knowing that the red of your car-flag is the blood of our people who fought for us.

'But now we fight for ourselves and those to come. Aluta continua. Fees must fall.'

We certainly had a special, historic edition of the *Cape Argus* on our hands and the sales showed that the following day, on 23 October 2015. It would set the tone for how, under my editorship, the paper would tackle issues in a way that would make the newsmakers the storytellers. We followed it up with The Dignity Project and that too was a rip-roaring success.

Was this not the antidote to falling newspaper sales and circulations? Unfortunately, I didn't have the chance to hang around long enough to find out, because I was soon moved within the company to the role of Regional Executive Editor and no longer had any real say in editorial decisions.

But I keenly tracked the progress of our original co-editor Ameera Conrad, who had made such a big impression on Lance and me when we first saw her delivering her poem under the big tree at UCT's Lower Campus. Exactly a year after that historic newspaper edition, Ameera went on to write, direct and star in a theatre production called *The Fall* – a stage narrative of the student uprisings of 2015, which made its debut at the Baxter Theatre. Universities in South Africa were again burning, and campuses had been shut down for weeks.

A then 23-year-old Ameera was back at the *Cape Argus*, but this time to talk about *The Fall*. She had graduated cum laude in 2015 with a BA in theatre and performance from UCT's drama department. But it was a year that shook her consciousness and that of thousands of other students like her, forever shaping the way she thinks.

'We found ourselves in a place where we, as students of colour, knew the buildings were not designed for us to be there in the first place. We all know Cecil John Rhodes donated the land for a university, but we also know that he donated the land for a university for white Englishmen to get good, quality education – even in the heart of deepest, darkest Africa,' she told me in an interview in 2016.

'We felt, I suppose, collectively as students of colour, that not enough was done to include us in the very fabric of UCT, because desegregation isn't transformation. We wanted to push for ourselves to be seen and heard in the space that we've been allowed into and claim it as our own.

'Going through #RhodesMustFall and then #FeesMustFall and (trying to) end outsourcing was quite difficult, because you become blind to these things until you're made aware of them. I think I was in that position at first.

'It was normal to me that people who looked like me were not on the walls. Books about people like me were not being studied, because that's just the way it is. Until the #RhodesMustFall movement shook the foundations of UCT, I was blissfully unaware that I was being excluded in some ways.'

As a graduate, Ameera found herself in a world not much different.

'The issue of not having a channel of work made by people of colour is exactly what I, and the people I'm working with on *The Fall*, are trying to overcome,' she said.

'We're in the position where we've been given the space and told to tell the story the way we want to tell it. Be as aggressive as you want to; be as quiet as you want to. Do it the way you feel most comfortable doing and help to contribute and create the work you think is missing from the theatre industry.

'It started halfway through last year, when the UCT drama department saw the need for more South African texts to be done and, kind of ironically, even before #RhodesMustFall was calling for more South African work, the drama department was planning on doing a Barney Simon season. Of course, Barney Simon directed and curated a lot of the seminal activist works that happened in South Africa during the 1980s and 1990s.'

What struck me more was just how decisive Ameera and her fellow student co-editors of that special edition were. A former deputy editor and friend, Yunus Kemp, used to repeat the phrase, 'My indecision is final.' It became a bit of a running gag when I couldn't make up my mind about what the paper should lead with. But here were a group of students, who we had dismissed as disengaged, on point and on the pulse of all that was wrong with our society.

A year later, Ameera reflected on that special edition of the *Cape Argus* and the year that was: 'I definitely think there is a raised consciousness. There was this notion that my generation is just here for the tweets. We're just here for the memes and LOLs. But, even through that, we've managed to engage in a new way.

'There is going to be something – even if it's not physical activism, even if it's a more social or intellectual activism – that will come from last year.

'To think that high school students are protesting their right to wear their hair the way they want to. When I was in high school, I didn't know that I was being discriminated against when I was told, "Your hair is wild; please plait it and keep it out of your face. It's the way the school works. Just do it and just get through."

'But actually, one can't just put one's head down anymore. I think it's inspiring to see young people, and young women of colour especially, standing up and saying we refuse to be treated differently because of the way we were born. We refuse to be born into disadvantage.'

With *The Fall*, Ameera and her stage colleagues wanted to move people in the same way the student-edited *Cape Argus* moved readers. 'We want people to see the behind-the-scenes, in the same way that we came to the *Cape Argus* to co-edit. That was an opportunity to tell our own stories and to show that we're not hooligans who just want to tear things down,' she said. 'We have a plan. It's just that part of the plan is that you have to remove the structures to put the new structures in place. You wouldn't build a new house on top of an old house where the foundations are cracking. It's really an opportunity for audience members to look behind the closed doors.

'It's weird, because when we started, we thought it would be a play aimed at the students to encourage or show support for them. But we've come to the point where it's actually become a play that's for the older generation, to tell them, "Don't worry: it's not Armageddon." The country is not going to end up in civil war in the next year. There are thinkers in movements. There are intellectuals and academics who are the leaders of the future.

'People are so quick to forget that Nelson Mandela started off as an intellectual and became militant because that is where you are pushed, where militancy is the only option for now, and once we've gone past that stage, the phase for reconciliation comes.'

I was invited to London the year after that memorable #ShutItDown student co-edited *Cape Argus* to receive an award from the International News and Media Association (INMA) for innovation in newspaper publishing. During the INMA conference preceding the awards, it was great standing in front of a group of my peers and describing how we went about publishing the edition. The idea of this democratic style of editing and collaborative storytelling resonated with the audience and afterwards I chatted with a number of editors from all over the world who were seeking advice on how to change the way we run our business. I half-jokingly told them that I'd be back the following year to pick up another award because, at the time, The Dignity Project (about the homeless in our society) was in the works.

I am fortunate to now work at an institution of higher learning where, as a media manager, I have the chance to engage with a host of the brightest young minds in our country. If given the chance, they can provide all the answers. And they're asking all the right questions as we flirt with the Fourth Industrial Revolution without taking a step back to consider the ethical consequences, like job losses and how technology should be aiding human development and not replacing it.

I am grateful too to Ameera Conrad, Dela Gwala, Leila Khan, Brian Kamanzi, Mbali Matandela, Amanda Xulu, Busisiwe Nxumalo, Simon Rakei and the rest of the university Class of 2015 for challenging my lazy thinking about South Africa and about the media space. They proved to me that, contrary to popular belief, you can edit a newspaper democratically. Okay, not always. But the most profound thing I learnt was that the constructs of society are constantly changing and we need to be open to and tolerant of that change. Furthermore, artificial hierarchy is the enemy of free thought.

Five years on, I look back at that student co-edited edition of *Cape Argus* and hold it up as my finest moment as a newspaper editor, and perhaps my entire career in journalism. Ironically, I was but a small cog in the making of that historic edition of a newspaper. All the credit is due to my student co-editors.

Also, I wasn't fired.

ASHLEY KRIEL
(1966 - 1987)

THE PRIDE OF
BONTEHEUWEL

 **Cape Argus** ▮ INDEPENDENT

16 June 2016. A special edition *Cape Argus* Youth Day poster featuring slain uMkhonto
we Sizwe activist Ashley Kriel to commemorate the 40th anniversary of June 16 in the
suburb of Bonteheuwel on the Cape Flats, where he proved to be a thorn in the side of
the security police. Design: Rowan Abrahams. ©*Independent Media*

7 Injustice

'In this new era, the *Cape Argus* newspaper's way of reporting, comparing it to back then, during the apartheid years – it went through my mind that at the time when they reported on Ashley's death in the *Cape Argus* it was said that Ashley was a terrorist. They branded Ashley a terrorist,' said the woman sitting across the table from me. Then she repeated it to drive the point home: 'A terrorist.'

I seldom struggle for words, but those few words left me dumbstruck. They shook me to the core and it took a while for me to compose myself. The woman who had uttered the words had looked me directly in the eyes, but she was now in tears and inconsolable.

The Ashley that Michel Assure was talking about was her brother Ashley Kriel. At the time of his murder, Ashley was a 20-year-old activist from Bonteheuwel, whom the apartheid government saw as such a threat that he became one of their most wanted targets. He was violently mowed down and it was claimed that his murder was an accident. But this was no accident, and more than three decades later, Michel and the rest of Ashley's family still seek answers about what happened to their younger brother, whom they last saw when he was just 17 years old.

The murder scene is a house in Albermarle Street in Hazendal, Athlone. It still stands – eerily as modest and unassuming now as it was on that fateful day of 9 July 1987. It was the day Ashley Kriel was killed.

The version of what happened recounted by Jeffrey Benzien – the infamous security policeman who used the 'wet-bag' method as part of his repertoire to torture activists – to the Truth and Reconciliation Commission (TRC), was that he shot 20-year-old Ashley by accident during a scuffle in the house. Benzien was granted amnesty, even though the TRC found that 'there are inconsistencies and even contradictions on some aspects'. He was granted amnesty on February 17, 1999.

From early on, my journalism career (which began at *The Star* newspaper in 1997 as a student intern aged 19) was punctuated with stories of bodies being exhumed – young men and women who bravely gave their lives, and who were tortured and brutally butchered by the apartheid security police. Their families lived in hope that they had skipped the country, had been living in exile and would return as our new democracy was born. Instead, their remains were exhumed so that their families could finally lay their sons and daughters to rest with dignity.

The family of Ashley Kriel was able to bury their son in a day of high drama in Bonteheuwel, as shown in the video footage taken on that day in 1987. The Cape Flats suburb was packed with activists, Struggle luminaries like Allan Boesak and Desmond Tutu, and an almost military-like presence in the form of the apartheid government's enforcers.

Elsewhere, decades before Ashley's funeral, an imam who had spoken out against apartheid from his mosque in Claremont was given a dignified burial at the Mowbray Muslim burial site near Groote Schuur Hospital on the slopes of Devil's Peak. Imam Haron Abdullah was killed in police detention in 1969 because he was seen as a threat to the apartheid government. The government also claimed the imam's death was an accident.

The imam's namesake, a young artist named Haroon Gunn-Salie, would later immortalise that funeral in one of his many exhibitions that pay tribute to the imam. Gunn-Salie had a strong connection to the imam, as he too was tormented as a toddler while incarcerated with his activist mother Shirley Gunn.

Between the decades of the imam's funeral – and closer to the death of Ashley Kriel's funeral – a son had some memories of his father, Fort Calata's, funeral. They were just bits and pieces of his recollections of that day. Fort was a member of a group of anti-apartheid activists known as the Cradock Four, who were killed by an apartheid hit squad. Part of the reason his son Lukhanyo became a journalist was to investigate the murder of the Cradock Four and bring the men responsible for their murder to justice. Ironically, in a democratic South Africa, Lukhanyo would face his own round of persecution.

These were but three accounts among scores of injustices that the TRC glossed over. Ashley Kriel's killer, Benzien, is still a free man, despite the overwhelming evidence that he murdered the young activist.

Lukhanyo's investigation culminated in a book entitled *My Father Died for This*, which he co-wrote with his journalist wife, Abigail Calata. The couple uncovered evidence that apartheid's senior government officials had given the green light for the hit on Fort Calata, Matthew Goniwe, Sicelo Mhlauli and Sparrow Mkhonto. Decades later, and despite the promises to re-open the case made by prosecutors and cabinet ministers in a democratic South Africa – some of whom were comrades of the Cradock Four – Lukhanyo is still fighting for justice.

The Abdullah family have had to live with the token gesture of having a street named after the imam, despite strong evidence that he was killed.

But back in the boardroom with Ashley Kriel's sister, Michel, I remained silent as I listened to her story of her family's years of torment as night after night the security police came looking for her brother. I wasn't even supposed to be at this meeting, but I was invited to join in after my own meeting at the corporate offices of Independent Media, the owners of the *Cape Argus*, on the foreshore of the Cape Town CBD, was cancelled.

The media company had made a commitment to part-fund the completion of a documentary about Ashley's life and murder, called *Action Kommandant*. The documentary was being directed by a talented young filmmaker and storyteller, Nadine Cloete – one of the first people Ashley's family were prepared to open up to – because of her sincerity and the respect she had for their son.

On that Tuesday, 23 February 2016, I faced a TRC of my own. Holding back her tears, Michel reflected on the way the *Cape Argus* had reported on Ashley's death. It was humbling to hear her thoughts and I was immersed in her story. Soon, Michel was in tears. Her emotional account was so raw and heartfelt, her pain so real, that it was as if Ashley had died just the day before. By then, I was choking back tears of my own.

'Ashley was very young when he was murdered. He started becoming active at a very young age – when he was about 14. When he died, I thought the security police were shit-scared of Ashley,' she said, while still looking at me despite there being several other people in that boardroom.

'They couldn't stand the fact that he was so young and so resilient. They killed Ashley and I know it. I went to the house where Ashley was killed and I could see – all the signs were there. They brutally tortured him. When I entered the house, I found blood on the tarmac in the backyard. On the stoep[12], I found blood. When I entered the kitchen, I found a trail of blood on the floor and on the walls. In the bathroom, I found a laundry basket with blood-stained clothing. I found, on another spot in the yard, a blood-stained cap. I found a towel, also blood-stained. In the backyard. I found a spade, also with blood on this spade. I painted this picture to myself.

'I was alone at home when the security police came to tell us about Ashley's death. It was very inhuman, the way they just came to tell us. First it was that Ashley killed himself; he shot himself. Then they just asked me so abruptly, "Who can go with you to go and identify him?"

'I was alone at home with my baby son. I just couldn't believe what they were telling me. I knew the brutality of the security police. We got to learn it during that time – what the security police would do sometimes to torture the people or to harass people.

'I just didn't believe that Ashley was dead. I thought they were playing a trick on me. When they left, I took my son with me and went to my neighbour down the road, a few doors away. He was also an activist and is now my brother-in-law. I went to tell the aunty that they just came to say Ashley is dead and that I had to go and identify him.

'I had to contact this captain at the Athlone Police Station. From there, Athlone Police Station referred me to the Salt River Mortuary. I went down that aisle in the Salt River Mortuary, still not believing that I was going to see my brother.

'When I last saw Ashley, he was 17-going-on-18. He was still my little brother and Ashley was very timid and still a boy. To me, he was my little brother, and walking down that aisle I thought: "You know what, I'm not going to see my little brother; it's not my brother."

'I thought: "The police are trying to play this trick on us. They're going to show me a mutilated body or something horrible just to unnerve me or just to do something bad, because that's what they did to the families."

'They used to do it to my mom. My mom was also so scared to death. They used to threaten her and said when they came looking for Ashley, "As ons hom kry gaan ons hom vrek skiet, plat skiet soos 'n haas." (If we find him, we'll gun him down like a hare).

'To think that at the end of the day they really carried out their threat. When I got to the end of that aisle in the mortuary, I got to this glass window, and when I saw him lying there all I could say to the aunty next to me was, "Shame, it is my little brother."

'But the first thing I noticed was on his forehead – a big gash. That's where the story comes in of what I saw in the yard: a bloodied spade. He was beaten with the spade. That's how those blood splatters came to be there. During that time when it was the death inquest – there wasn't even an exhibit of the stuff found at the scene.

'When we went to the TRC, only then could they send forensic people out and they could trace the blood stains, although the walls had been painted over. And they could trace the blood stains on that floor. I feel the TRC failed us, because the perpetrator never came clean; he never told the truth and he was granted amnesty.

'I'm a Christian. Even during the TRC hearings Jeffrey Benzien came to me and he extended his hand to me. I turned my back to him, because I couldn't find it in my heart to forgive him. He was never repentant, and he boasted about Ashley's death. I turned my back. I refused to shake his hand.

'Sometimes I feel so guilty. I always make this example when we speak about Madiba – such a remarkable man. He could find it in his heart to forgive those perpetrators. He sacrificed so many years. Ashley died in an instant. But Madiba also suffered. So, who am I not to want to forgive Benzien?

'But I still say if he had to come clean ... how he boasted and boasted about how he killed and tortured and interrogated other comrades. He boasted about Ashley's death. I still couldn't believe that, even after our newfound democracy, he was still employed in the police force.

'There were times I felt I wanted to do something to this man. I had many sleepless nights when I felt I wanted to go and kill him, because how could he kill my brother? My mom probably also didn't have the will to live. My father was taken when my mom was 29 and he was brutally stabbed to death. She had to rear us single-handedly. Then he still goes and takes her son?

'I felt that I wanted to go and kill him. I went to the extent where I went through a telephone directory and I found [his contact details]. I found his address. I thought: "Ag, if only I could get hold of a firearm or something and just one night ask someone to take me there."

'I thank God I came to my senses. They tortured and maimed us. They killed my little brother. But at the end of the day we came out stronger people.'

Michel Assure, like Ashley and the rest of her family, who still live in Bonteheuwel, is no ordinary woman. Lukhanyo Calata is no ordinary man. I thought he was; but I was wrong. In fact, Lukhanyo is exceptionally brave. Dare I say, if his father were alive today, he would be very proud. Courage runs in his blood.

Abigail Calata is no ordinary woman. Together with Lukhanyo, the journalist and author was prepared to sacrifice all they had, including the family's well-being, in support of her husband when he was fired from his job at the SABC for speaking out against injustice at the broadcaster.

I am an ordinary man. I flinch when confronted with adversity, even when I have the unequivocal support of an extraordinary woman – my wife Laylaa Abarder. But despite this unconditional and unwavering support, I would think several times before I put my livelihood at risk. I'm not a trust fund kid. Far from it; I'm one pay cheque away from losing everything. Lukhanyo and Abigail, who have a young son, aren't trust fund kids either. But the difference is they don't blink in the face of adversity. The couple earned my respect when the saga known as the #SABC8 unfolded.

I met Lukhanyo more than a decade before the #SABC8 drama and didn't really know who he was, except that he was a talented young broadcaster who had worked in both radio and TV journalism. Only later did I realise he was the son of Struggle activist Fort Calata – one of the Cradock Four who were assassinated by the apartheid regime's brutal machinery.

Lukhanyo doesn't go around telling people who his daddy was. Had it not been for two of my mentors, journalists Benny Gool and Roger Friedman, I may never have known about the link.

This context is important for what happened later. It was Monday, 27 June 2016. The SABC's peculiar boss, Hlaudi Motsoeneng, was creating havoc, ordering journalists to turn their cameras away from protests, among other ridiculous moves. Journalists who stood up against Hlaudi were fired. A core group, who came to be known as the #SABC8, were at the centre of the rebellion. Lukhanyo was part of this group, and was first summarily suspended and then dismissed.

It was an ordinary day in the *Cape Argus* newsroom when I got an extraordinary call that Monday. On the line was radio broadcaster, Koketso Sachane, a mutual friend of Lukhanyo and me. He said that Lukhanyo wanted to break his silence about Hlaudi's reign of terror. He was ready to stand in direct opposition to his bosses.

Lukhanyo was by then an accomplished and high-profile parliamentary correspondent for the SABC. The news value immediately dawned on me: Fort Calata's son was to walk in his father's footsteps against injustice.

I devoted big resources to the story, assigning deputy news editor Lance Witten to interview Lukhanyo. We brought in a video team and started broadcasting Lukhanyo's interview. It made an immediate impact.

The interview was splashed on the front page of the *Cape Argus* the next day, with the headline, 'Is this what Fort Calata died for?' The subhead read, 'Slain activist's son and SABC staffer hits out at his bosses'.

Lukhanyo told Lance in the interview: 'I made the decision to become a journalist after years of watching journalists coming to our home as part of their drive to tell the story about my father and his comrades. Thirty-one years later, I now work as a news reporter, with the sole purpose of telling the stories of my people with dedication, truth and freedom. A freedom that many like my father either died for or were imprisoned for.

'It is therefore with great sadness that I am confronted with the disturbing direction being taken by my employers; a direction that, I believe, flies in the face of (the ideals of) what many have sacrificed (their lives for).'

I was in awe of Lukhanyo's bravery. A few days later, Lukhanyo and Abigail showed even greater courage when they joined a group of journalists protesting outside the SABC's Sea Point offices in support of his colleagues. Days later, Lukhanyo was fired.

I called Lukhanyo after he was dismissed, feeling responsible because of the front page splash in the *Cape Argus*. He reassured me that he had done the right thing and would do it again if he needed to.

Fortunately, sanity prevailed and Lukhanyo was soon back at the SABC doing what he does best and reporting from Parliament. Hlaudi, fortunately, is no more and is pursuing his political ambitions – albeit Don Quixote-like.

On the face of it the Calatas are an ordinary couple – with bills and school runs, just like me. But they are doing extraordinary things. Their book, *My father died for this*, gives a heart-wrenching account of bullying and oppression. It is recommended reading for every South African.

Lukhanyo is steadfast in his resolve to honour his father, and his activist grandfather, James Calata, by working tirelessly to bring the Cradock Four's killers to book, and lobbying for the government's prosecuting authority to act. He won't rest. It is a selfless act on behalf of all of those who can't find the expression, the resources or the voice to find justice.

Thousands of people who now occupy the highest seats of power in a free South Africa were at the Cradock Four's funeral. Lukhanyo was but a little boy when his dad was buried, and didn't quite comprehend the enormity of the moment. It was a moment in the history of the Struggle that would be a turning point, as anger spilled over because of the murders. However, those self-same occupiers of the highest seats of power in a free South Africa now seem reluctant to act. It is as if they have forgotten and have betrayed the legacy of Fort Calata and his fallen comrades. In particular, Calata and Goniwe (both teachers), were instrumental in setting up the Cradock Residents Association and the Cradock Youth Association, and they refused to bow to the town council appointed for them in an undemocratic South Africa that oppressed the black residents of the area, and that was regarded as illegitimate. Instead, they set up an alternative form of people's governance, and their success became an embarrassment to the regime – an embarrassment that had to be eliminated, and the order came from the very top.

It was also a funeral that brought the pain and suffering of Imam Haron Abdullah's family to life for me through the art of the talented Haroon Gunn-Salie.

How do you bring to life the story of a man's death and his legacy when the circumstances are shrouded in mystery? You won't readily find accounts in textbooks or reference books of Imam Abdullah Haron – the anti-apartheid cleric, from Claremont's Stegman Road Mosque, who died after being tortured for 123 days in police detention in 1969.

There is a street in Lansdowne (a section of the old Lansdowne Road) named after Imam Haron. But it is a stark and lonely reminder of the imam's martyrdom in his fight against injustice and the significant role he played in our fight for liberation. The imam's crime was that he dared to preach against oppression.

Gunn-Salie was the keynote speaker at the commemoration ceremony on the 46th anniversary of the imam's death, held at his gravesite in Mowbray. Gunn-Salie was born exactly 20 years after the imam's death, but his life would become intrinsically linked to his namesake.

In 2015, Gunn-Salie celebrated his first solo exhibition as an artist at the Goodman Gallery in Joburg. It was called *History after Apartheid* and enjoyed critical acclaim. The most memorable of the pieces exhibited was a work entitled *Amongst Men*, which was dedicated to the late Imam Haron.

But it was his search for answers about his own childhood that started Gunn-Salie on his journey. Before he was even two years old, Gunn-Salie found himself in a prison cell, just like his namesake. Like Imam Haron, the young artist too had a history with Claremont. Both the cleric and Haroon's father and his family were forcibly removed from the suburb, which was declared a whites-only area under the apartheid Group Areas Act.

Born to parents – activists Shirley Gunn and Aneez Salie – who were both uMkhonto we Sizwe soldiers, Gunn-Salie lived in the underground from birth. Later, Shirley was arrested and the toddler was detained with her. Gunn-Salie was later removed from his mom and sent to a children's home. Security police played back recordings of the toddler crying to torment his mother.

'It was the driving force behind me getting involved in this sort of work. I don't have direct memory of it, but I have memory told through narrative. I think I'm able to retell my early childhood experience by being a witness; being retold a story as opposed to my own recollection, which is very important,' he told me in an interview for the *Cape Argus*.

'By the age of two, we had been released from prison and my mother and I were living with my dad's father in 2nd Avenue, Crawford – the house they were forcibly removed to from Claremont. I was playing in the front garden and a cat came by and I freaked out and started crying. I had never seen a cat before, and I was two years old. While my granddad was consoling me, a police van drove past and I started screaming: "The boere are here. We have to go inside to hide so they can't see us."

'I didn't know what a cat looked like, but I knew exactly what to do when the police came by. This is the uniqueness of experiencing something in utero. In those first two years, I had no interaction with children, so I could speak fluently because I had only seen adults. There was no normal early childhood development.'

Part of Gunn-Salie's fascination with Imam Haron was that he was named after him. The other part was that he and his mom, Shirley, could have suffered the same fate as the imam. But by then the mass democratic Struggle was able to take to the streets and mobilise. There were marches down Wale Street in the Cape Town CBD, with posters that read, 'Return Baby Haroon to Shirley'. 'It was the Cape Town Muslim community that largely petitioned for our release. There is very much a feeling of me being indebted,' said Gunn-Salie.

Gunn-Salie was reunited with his mom after Judge Siraj Desai, then an advocate, obtained a court order on his behalf. Gunn-Salie would be the youngest political prisoner in our dark history and Desai's youngest client, at 18 months old.

Amongst Men features the casts of more than 400 kufiyas (traditional Muslim headwear for men) suspended from the ceiling, representing the mourners who buried Imam Haron at the Muslim burial grounds in Mowbray.

'A man amongst men is someone raised to incredible stature; but there's also you as a viewer being able to walk in and your presence fulfils the scene. It's the scene of Iman Haron's funeral – more than 400 kufiyas hung at the exact height, the angle and tilt of all the men in attendance at his burial,' said the young artist.

'You are invited, as the viewer, to become one with the men – one of these people. It's essentially the opposite of a monument, because a monument makes a hero out of the individual. It's linear and high. This represents the mass: all the multitude of voices touched by the imam who came to attend his funeral, in this act of defiance.

'The kufiya became the marker, because it's the connection between the divine and the mortal. These points raised in the air were importantly taken from archive photographs, so the way they are hung is exactly to specifications. Because the brave photographers climbed up the trees that day and took these photographs from above, once again it comes down to these markers of public memory.

'The audio in the piece is a poem by James Matthews. He wrote the poem *Patriot or Terrorist* as part of his first anthology called *Cry Rage*. He was imprisoned for this literature. It's a piece that is as relevant today as when it was written in 1969, because it speaks to the global context of Islamophobia and hatred that is spread by people completely misguided by propaganda.

'James's poem is asking whether the imam was a patriot or a terrorist, and whether his martyrdom is there as an example or whether it is a crying shame. The audio is of him [James] as an 85-year-old performing this poem. It was always a written piece and never a recorded or performed piece. His words ring out above the people at the installation.'

Amongst Men led to two other pieces in collaboration with the imam's family. The second piece depicts Imam Haron's body, cast in Haroon's image and based on interviews with the imam's widow, Galiema. The third piece is a hand-blown lightbulb suspended at the height of a child, which was inspired by the interviews Haroon conducted with the imam's daughter, Fatiema Haron Masoet.

Like *Amongst Men*, Haroon's body of work is dominated by the highlighting of injustices of the past and how injustices continue in the present. As part of his *History after Apartheid* exhibition, Haroon cast the hands from actual statues of colonial figures of South Africa – including Cecil John Rhodes, Jan van Riebeeck and Paul Kruger – in red, depicting how they had blood on their hands.

Gunn-Salie's father, Aneez Salie, veteran journalist and former editor of the *Cape Times*, knew Ashley Kriel well. In fact, the two were best friends. Aneez, himself an uMkhonto we Sizwe soldier in training beyond our borders at the time, said Ashley was a talented young man who was earmarked to receive officer training all over the world, in countries sympathetic to the liberation Struggle. But Ashley became physically ill at the thought of not continuing his fight back home. At his insistence, the ANC eventually sent Ashley home after his military training was complete.

As Aneez Salie recalls: 'He felt so committed to our people, he was determined to offer his own life. Not recklessly, because there were none who loved life more than those who were prepared to give it up for a cause.

'In MK and the ANC, we got to know the greatest love there is; for what greater love can there be than to be prepared to give your life for another?'

Ashley went from exile straight back to the house where he and other activists would meet. It proved to be a fatal mistake. At the house in Albermarle Street in Hazendal, Athlone, Ashley Kriel was murdered on 9 July 1987. The family would read about it in the *Cape Argus* – that their son, 'the terrorist', had died accidently in a scuffle with police while resisting arrest.

However, David Klatzow, a renowned forensic investigator, said his own investigation concluded that Ashley was murdered by Benzien. At the time Nadine Cloete's documentary was launched, there was lots of noise being made by the police's elite investigating unit (the Hawks) about re-opening the case. That was four years ago, but nothing has happened since. Benzien is still a free man.

Michel's story shook me to the core. I had only recently started learning about Ashley's story. I knew he had left his community in Bonteheuwel at a young age to join the ANC's military wing Umkhonto we Sizwe.

But that day, 23 February 2016, I was determined to set matters right at my own TRC. The media had played a massive role in the disinformation campaigns that furthered the aims of the apartheid government. Some of my predecessors at the *Cape Argus* and at other newspapers had blood on their hands and were complicit in the evil atrocities committed by the apartheid security police – either by omission or commission. They aided and abetted the regime with the help of cover-ups or propaganda. Some of these same media figures now claim to be the guardians of the free press.

That Tuesday morning, I offered my apology to Michel and her family. Later, in a piece on my encounter with Michel at that meeting, and as then editor of the *Cape Argus*, I offered my unconditional apology to all those the newspaper had wronged, because it had, in some way, however small, indirectly or directly, supported a regime that thought nothing of taking the life of a young man such as Ashley Kriel and so many others.

Just the year before, we learnt that a former Sunday Times editor, Tertius Myburgh, an almost legendary figure in South African journalism, had been an apartheid spy. That same year, Media24's then Chief Executive, Esmare Weideman, apologised for Naspers' role in supporting the apartheid regime.

I was also able to write about the injustice and oppression dished out by my very own company, the then Independent Newspapers, against my then colleague, Aneez Salie, and many other black journalists – long after our hard-won democracy was born.

Etched as part of the painful memories and hurt Michel suffered, losing her brother Ashley so violently, is how the *Cape Argus* branded him a 'terrorist' and callously reported the triumph of the security police at the time. It took the bravery of a young filmmaker, Nadine Cloete, to remind all of us at the *Cape Argus* headquarters, Newspaper House, that Ashley's story had not been told properly, and that my children and their children needed to know the truth.

And to my profession I ask: where is the TRC for the media who aided and abetted apartheid?

16 November 2018. Desiree Ellis, head coach of South Africa, during the national women's team Banyana Banyana's training session at the Nduom Sports Stadium in Ghana. Photo: Sydney Mahlangu. *©BackpagePix/ANA Pictures*

8 *Trailblazers*

'C'mon boys,' says the coach, as a group of 7-year-olds are taken through their paces during a football drill. It looks like a group of boys at first glance. But in the middle of the group is a kid with shoulder-length hair and in a full Manchester United replica kit, who immediately walks despondently off the pitch.

'I can't do this, dad. I don't like it here,' my daughter Misha tells me. And that's the end of that. Another football club that doesn't accommodate girls. If you're a girl and want to play soccer, you have to assimilate and play with the boys. It's not that she can't do what the boys do. It's the language the coach chose to use, knowing full well she was there, that made her throw in the towel. The coach meanwhile is oblivious, looking puzzled as to why we chose to leave.

Welcome to the world of every woman who has ever walked into a boardroom filled with men and needed to somehow prove themselves or find a way to be heard. I became acutely aware too when I was the only man in a meeting with women, debating a marketing campaign, just how awful it is when the roles are reversed. I became uncharacteristically quiet. I am conscious of my behaviour, too, as the struggle to find a girls-only football team for my daughter opened my eyes to this daily discrimination that men just don't see.

But almost 50 years ago, when this planet was very much a man's world – more so than it is today – a 7-year-old who grew up in Salt River was showing the girls and boys how it's done with her football. In 1969, it was unheard of for a girl to play football. But Desiree Ellis would become South Africa's most celebrated and pioneering women's footballer, and would eventually lead the national team to a Women's African Cup of Nations final and the holy grail – a first ever participation in the FIFA Women's World Cup.

I have been a committed soccer fan from the age of 11 when a classmate of my older sister first told me the stories of a young footballer who would become a pioneer of the game. My sister's classmate would also influence me to become a lifelong Manchester United fan, supplying me with a hand-me-down home-and-away kit from the 1988/89 season (that I now regret giving away, since I've become a football kit collector).

The following year, I had my first taste of the FIFA World Cup with Italia '90 – the World Cup of Paul 'Gazza' Gascoigne, Salvatore 'Toto' Schillaci and Lothar Matthäus. I became hooked on 'the beautiful game'.

But the young footballer who sparked my love for soccer wasn't Gazza, Schillaci or Matthäus. The player wasn't male either. That young footballer was my sister's classmate's sister, Desiree – a founding member of the South African national women's soccer team, Banyana Banyana, and its eventual captain for more than a decade.

I could easily identify with Desiree's story, the girl from Salt River who would not let the fact that there was no girls' team in those days dampen her enthusiasm for following a career in soccer. Desiree and I – albeit a few years apart – went to the same schools (Dryden Street Primary School and Salt River High School), played soccer in the same streets, and knew the stories of the same local Salt River soccer heroes, like brothers Ismail and Siraaj Abbas.

If I had odds stacked against me (mostly due to my limited soccer-playing ability), then Desiree had a mountain to climb, growing up in world of patriarchy. But that did little to stop her from reaching the highest peaks of the women's game.

'I grew up in Salt River as we stayed at my late grandmother's house after school. We regularly played against boys from the surrounding streets around Greef Street,' she told me in an interview about a year before her appointment as the coach for the national women's team in 2015.

'I used to regularly go with my late father to most of the local games, and also the Cape Town City and Hellenic derbies. I always watched local football whenever I had the opportunity, and watching at Shelley Road springs to mind.

'I mostly played with my boy cousins and even played cricket. Street football was the best though, but our game stopped when people left their places of work in the evening and walked down Greef Street to get to Salt River train station.

'Well, that's where it all started, playing football in the boys' playground at Dryden Street Primary. I always jumped over the fence to play football with the boys, but also played netball for the school and missed out on detention.

'I later attended Salt River High School, and still there was no football for girls. I participated in netball, hockey and athletics. I ended up playing for the teachers' side every year against the school team, made up of boys, and that's where I got scouted to play for my first club, Athlone Celtic.'

It was a to and fro affair for Desiree to play competitive football in the late 1970s and 1980s. She joined Athlone Celtic in 1978 and played there until 1984, when the club closed down. She then joined Wynberg St Johns for a year before she and her teammates formed their own club, called Joyces United, in 1986. In 1988, Desiree joined Moonlighters for a year, before starting another new team with her teammates (St Albans). In 1990, she returned to Joyces United, which became Saban United. She later joined Cape Town Spurs, until they merged with Seven Stars and became Ajax Cape Town.

Desiree and her teammates would eventually form Spurs Women's Football Club – a club with which she would become synonymous.

But her adventure as a top-level footballer was only just beginning.

The Laureus Sport Foundation describes her as a legend. Desiree made her international debut for Banyana Banyana against Swaziland at the age of 30 in 1993. The next year, she would become captain of the side, and would lead Banyana Banyana until the day she retired in April 2002.

Her Laureus citation reads: 'A midfielder, Ellis led the way in helping raise the profile of women's football in South Africa. When the country hosted the African Women's Championship in 2000, she skippered the side to a runners-up finish.

'Ellis was given recognition for her services to soccer in the same year when she received a Silver Presidential Sports Award. In 2002, she led Banyana Banyana to the Cosafa (Council of Southern Africa Football Associations) Cup title.

'During her time in the South Africa team she enjoyed tremendous success, winning 23 matches, losing just seven and drawing two ... Ellis is one of the few individuals to have captained a football team for an entire decade, playing 32 matches and winning 23 of those – a win rate of 72 per cent.

'Her standing in South African football was made clear when she was chosen to be an ambassador for the FIFA World Cup when it was hosted in her home country in 2010.'

Desiree has not stopped working on her game and is now also a broadcaster and commentator.

'I'm continuing to live my dream, and to top it all, I'm still involved in the beautiful game. It's very demanding, though, as I watch lots of games on TV and even watch local NFD and Ajax Cape Town games,' she said.

'I do lots of research, not only on players, but on clubs as well. And doing coaching courses has improved my knowledge of the game.'

The women's game has changed considerably for the better since the days when Desiree was playing.

'Back in the day, we only had one league and got selected for provincial teams, and that's where eventually we got selected for Banyana Banyana.

'Now we have the Sasol league in nine provinces, consisting of about 16 teams, and regional leagues in almost all of the regions, as well as under-13 and under-15 at LFA football.

'A lot has been done, but there is always more that can be done. Make no mistake, without the sponsorship our football would be non-existent. We need to have the best playing against the best every week, and this will improve the quality of play and also make for a better national team.

With Desiree as a mentor, the women's game in South Africa is in good hands. Laureus was not being overly generous when it described the woman who started honing her skills on the streets of Salt River as a legend. Based on some of her achievements, Desiree's career was made in football heaven. She is a national treasure.

She won numerous awards along the way, and it was on her watch that Banyana Banyana qualified to play in their first World Cup in France in 2019. It would see one of her players, Thembi Kgatlana, score a historic first goal against favourite, Spain, in South Africa's first group match. The year before, under Desiree's management, Thembi was named African Women's Footballer of the Year. Thembi now plays for FC Benfica in Portugal and in the women's Champions

League. Almost a dozen more players whom Desiree has mentored now play for some of the world's biggest football clubs.

Another trailblazer in a man's world is my former colleague, Julia Stuart. Or better known to the team at the *Daily Voice*, when she was editor there, as the 'soccer *meisie*[13] with balls'. A few months after joining the *Daily Voice*, as the only woman among the sports journos, it became abundantly clear that she was destined for bigger things. Julia made it her business to learn layout, design and editing, and never stopped asking questions. She had a furious work ethic and soon started her own column. The footballers, coaches and fellow sports writers slowly but surely started to respect Julia's skills as one of the country's leading football writers. She became sports editor of the *Daily Voice* at the age of just 22.

When *eNCA* head-hunted her as a sports reporter and later anchor, Julia took to the task like a duck to water. Later still, she would headline SuperSport's massively popular *Monday Night Football*, and is often seen pitchside at some of the biggest local and international matches.

In 2016, Julia called it very confidently that Leicester City would be crowned English Premier League champions – creating the biggest sports story of the year. No, scratch that: the decade! It's one of the reasons I don't take Julia on easily when it comes to football. I learnt more than a decade ago she has few peers when it comes to knowledge of the beautiful game.

The story of Leicester City is a good metaphor for Julia's own rise to presenter of SuperSport's *Monday Night Football*. Julia has the job that many lads dream of. She got it through sheer hard work, determination and old-fashioned values.

'We kept expecting Leicester to slip up. Everyone said they would never ever survive. They just kept doing it, they just kept surprising us. All of us who support football would like to see about a tenth of that in the sides we support,' she said when I caught up with her years after she had left the *Daily Voice*.

'It just makes it seem anything is possible, especially in the Premier League where it's all about money and big-name players. Leicester don't really have that. It's the story that has given us all belief, and it's inspiring in the modern day, because it says that all those old principles and values we don't think have a place in modern day are still very much valid.'

I met Julia just over a decade ago when I was news editor of the *Daily Voice*. She was studying when she started working as a sports writer, then layout sub at the newspaper. Like so many success stories at the *Daily Voice*, she was another of the 'strays' brought in by then-editor, Karl Brophy. Karl had a knack for finding diamonds, and he saw something in Julia when he spoke to a group of students about the paper.

'I was studying film and media when Karl gave a lecture at UCT. I walked up to him afterwards. I was working for the UCT newspaper and with the World Cup 2010 on the horizon, I had made a decision that I was going into sports, and that there was going to be scope. I went to Karl and said: "I want a job",' she said.

'I consider myself very lucky in my career. They say the harder you work the more luck you seem to find yourself getting. A couple of people had left the *Daily Voice* and I was just there in the right place at the right time, I guess. It was also a case of getting that opportunity and literally just working so hard and trying not to let anyone down.

'I was given this huge responsibility and was probably the youngest sports editor in the country at 22.'

Karl's successor, Elliott Sylvester, current editor Taariq Halim and I, as then deputy editor, would benefit from Karl's intuition. Julia was a gem at the *Daily Voice* and brought the sports pages to life on a daily basis.

'I learnt from you guys, especially you and Elliott, because you were right there at the beginning. I thought these two guys are so cool; they know everything about everything. You were extremely intimidating and Elliott was more approachable,' she said. 'You're working with these two young cool cats of the South African newspaper world. You just want to learn and you want to be up there and not let them down.

'For a long time, I was given opportunities while I was at the *Daily Voice* to do TV and radio as a guest analyst. A lot of people asked why didn't I leave sooner, but I think that was always home for me. I always felt that I didn't write for the *Daily Voice* just because I had to. I still feel some attachment to the paper.'

But we knew Julia was destined for a bigger platform. (Personally, I believe she could do a better job coaching Arsenal than any current manager. And her one flaw, if she has one, is that she's an Arsenal fan.)

Julia was born and raised in Mitchells Plain. Her parents divorced when she was still young and, although she's her mom's only child, she has two sisters from her dad and step-mom.

She attended York Road Primary in Lansdowne then went to Livingstone High, where she caused a stir when she announced she was taking a gap year after school. But once Julia makes up her mind, it is hard to sway her resolve. Her mom, in particular, wasn't sure she was making the right move when she decided to leave the *Daily Voice* for *eNCA*. 'It was such a big risk because I took a big pay cut. But I just thought, it's time to move and challenge myself. I had been at the newspaper for so long – I think it was seven years.

'I remember my mom was very skeptical because she thought it was a lot of money and she wondered how could I leave because I was a sports editor then, and now I was going to be a junior? But I thought, nothing ventured, nothing gained.

'It is intimidating being in front of a camera, and when I watch those first few tapes of mine from *eNCA*, I just cringe. It's hard to watch yourself on TV. The first few tapes you do, oh, those are horrible!'

But Julia usually aces everything she attempts. Within six months at the channel she was given the chance to anchor the sports bulletins.

'I found I was so much better as an anchor because I had that background of being an editor. People think you sit there and read, but in the Cape Town office you produce your own bulletin and write your own story, while editing other people's writing a little bit for your voice. That gave me incredible experience and I could also lean on the experience I had as a sports editor at the newspaper.'

Julia quickly became a household name. But what she wanted was to be involved in football. At the time, SuperSport had wanted a cricket presenter, and later a rugby presenter. But Julia wasn't interested.

'What happened with SuperSport is I hounded them. I didn't want to be just another woman because they needed a woman. I felt that you can put me in any football stadium or ask me about any football league around the world and I'd be able to tell you something. I was passionate about football and I knew that would translate, so I just bided my time.

'I remember the morning of the Currie Cup Final in 2014, I met the head of production at SuperSport, Alvin Naicker, at the hotel where the Western Province team was staying. Alvin kept saying they were looking for a rugby person.

'At the time, all the rugby coaches, like Paul Treu and Allister Coetzee, and the players, were coming to greet me. He kept saying: "Are you sure you don't want to do rugby; you have rugby contacts?"

'I said: "No, I want to do football."

'Once I had that meeting with him it happened very quickly. I flew to Joburg one Monday and did my interview and got a contract. The rest is history. But it was very daunting.

'My contract was split between reporting for *Blitz* and live football. The *Blitz* reporting I took to like a duck to water, because it's the same as what I had been doing for years. But live sports! SuperSport just dropped me into the deep end. I went from shadowing one game with Kamza Mbatha and that was on the Wednesday – by the Saturday I was on air.

But Julia also learnt quickly about the challenge of being a woman in a male-dominated world. 'The first interview I ever did, I'll never forget. The coach was so rude to me. The first question was answered with an, "If you know football …"

'I just wanted to cry and come back home thinking I'm never going to hack it. It happens every time I go to a local game. I get approached by women, young and old, and I think that is a reminder constantly to me that you are not in the majority.

'You're constantly walking a tightrope. Our bosses believe in us and they give us scope. To them it's not a case of you're just a woman. They're empowering us. They're sending people like Crystal Arnold and Elma Smit to the World Cup. Motshidisi Mohono went to the Laureus Awards. We're capable and they know that.

'But out there, people are constantly reminding you that you are a woman. We are in 2016 and it shouldn't be like that. But we perpetuate this culture that any woman can be a sports presenter because they don't need to know sport. That's nonsense, because it makes it harder for women like myself, who do actually know their sport, who are passionate about it, to be taken seriously.'

Julia was particularly irate about the unsavoury incident involving Chris Gayle and female TV journalist, Mel McLaughlin, during Australia's T20 Big Bash league in 2016. Gayle started making unbecoming remarks to McLaughlin on live TV. 'You see something like the Chris Gayle thing happening and people say, "Oh, it was only a joke." It's not a joke – the men who came out to support Chris Gayle in the wake of that situation. It's a big deal. You're telling the rest of the world to hit on this woman and to belittle her. She's just doing her job, but because she's a woman "… it's okay and everyone is going to back me. My team is going to pay my fine for me. It doesn't matter. I don't care."

'I always think, how does Chris Gayle's wife feel sitting at home? It's a battle we're constantly fighting and it makes me sick that Frank Sinatra in 1970-whatever was treated worse for being sexist at a concert than Chris Gayle was in 2016. Have we actually moved forward?'

It's hard to believe Julia is only in her 30s. What's next for the 'soccer *meisie* with balls'?

'I want to have sustainability in this industry. I want to be at the top. I want to get to the level of the Robert Marawas and Carol Tshabalalas. I feel like I'm still learning and have so much to learn because touch-line presenting is so different and live studio presenting is so different to anchoring. I'm still a baby in broadcasting.

'As a woman, there are other things to think about as well. I want to have a family – and then can I be travelling to Polokwane on a Saturday and Nelspruit on a Sunday when I have kids at home? Probably not; so there are those things to think about as well.

'I'll have to morph and learn other skills. I'm an example of that modern woman who's going to be 35, 36 or 37 when she has a kid.

'I will do it in the way that my life is meant to be done. I don't know how that is, it will just work out the way it's meant to work out. But maybe you'll see me anchoring on *CNN* or *ESPN*. I won't rule that out.'

Kass Naidoo and Natalie Germanos are also at the top of their game as TV and radio commentators for SABC cricket matches. The duo regularly travel abroad to cover international tournaments. It is so disappointing then that SuperSport, despite its success with Julia covering football and Cato Louw covering rugby, have no women involved in their cricket commentary teams. This is short-sighted. Including an experienced broadcaster like Kass would provide a fantastic addition to any all-male commentary team.

Elsewhere, women in our country are breaking the glass ceiling. For them, there is no ceiling. The University of the Western Cape's (UWC) Professor Mmaki Jantjies and Dr Fanelwa Ngece-Ajayi, two of South Africa's leading women in Science, Technology, Engineering and Mathematics (STEM), collaborated with Dr Sebolelo Mokapela, of the university's isiXhosa department. The trio successfully translated the periodic table into isiXhosa to encourage mother tongue chemistry instruction, while introducing blended learning in lectures with augmented reality on smartphones. At UWC too, the Springbok women's team captain, Babalwa Latsha, who hails from Khayelitsha, graduated with an LLB degree in 2019. In early 2020, she became the first South African woman to sign for a professional women's rugby side in Europe. 'I think that women's sport across the board could be better supported financially, so that we are able to make a proper living out of sport, because we love sport,' she said of her signing as SA's first professional women's rugby player. 'Dream big, because dreams do come true, but work hard towards that dream, so that when the opportunity comes, it finds you ready and fit in all aspects. We grow up in disadvantaged communities where, statistically, we are bound to fail. But the key thing is to keep the hope alive that one day things will change.'

In a Women's Month special edition of UWC's official sports magazine (Blue and Gold), Babalwa wrote about the challenges of being a trailblazer in a male-dominated world.

'I draw inspiration from Caster Semenya and Serena Williams. These are women who are ground breakers, who are not afraid to live their truth, who break all stereotypes and refuse to accept mediocrity as the norm – so much so that the world is starting to listen and speak a different narrative because of them. I train extremely hard and have built my physique to be able to handle the rigorous sport of rugby and to compete with elite athletes. Yet I am ridiculed and sometimes ostracised, even by other women.'

So, where to for my young daughter Misha, the 7-year-old aspiring footballer? If some of the women at the top of their game in their chosen field of expertise are still fighting for equality, should I be more protective of her? Shall we just keep looking for a football club she can assimilate into and play with and against the boys because no football association has thought it necessary to develop the game by bringing younger girls, under the age of 10, into a league of their own? There are now under-12 and under-14 leagues, but this is no consolation for my daughter whose favourite footballer is Manchester United's Marcus Rashford. She has no women's football role model like Thembi Kgatlana, because the women's game gets hardly any exposure on television or the media.

We kept being told to let her play with the boys and then when she is under-12 she can play in an all-girls team. That's not good enough. It's not good enough in a country that has competed in its first FIFA Women's World Cup and produced our first African Women's Footballer of the Year. This, despite there being no pro-fessional women's league in South Africa. It is a national disgrace, and the administrators of the game who give lip service to women's football should hang their heads in shame.

It's no accident that the US women's national soccer team are the current FIFA Women's World Cup champions. It is said that there are about 450 000 women and girl footballers playing at different levels of competition and across age groups in the US. The college game, in particular, is massive. This is why the US will dominate the women's game for many more years to come – because there is a plan and investment in women's football.

Coincidently, African Women's Footballer of the Year for 2019, Thembi Kgatlana, also hails from UWC, where the women's team enjoys more resources than the men's game, thanks to the visionary leadership of the University's Director of Sport, Mandla Gagayi. Gagayi says that, on his watch, he will be striving for all women's sporting codes to be managed and coached by women.

For now, at least, Misha is content to have a kick-about with me and her older brother Ziyaad, who also plays football. For her, it's all about being on the field and improving her ball skills. She loves nothing more than putting on her kit and boots, trying to mimic

Ziyaad's every move or trying out something she saw Marcus Rashford do on TV.

And every time Misha asks me when she'll be able to play for a club, my football heart breaks a bit more. I then tell her about Desiree Ellis, Julia Stuart, Prof. Mmaki Jantjies, Dr Funelwa Ngece-Ajayi, Dr Sebolelo Mokapela and Babalwa Latsha, who let no challenge stand in their way. She'll respond by saying, 'Dad, it's okay. I just want to be a firefighter.'

I smile and then my heart is full again. I'm determined to start a girls-only league for under 10s and younger – not just for Misha, but because it's the right thing to do. Watch this space.

4 November 2016. Former Proteas 'A' team and senior bowling coach Vincent Barnes showing the Independent Media's Regional Executive Editor Gasant Abarder the correct grip for batting during a trial to see whether Abarder had what it takes to be a Proteas cricketer. Photo: Cindy Waxa. ©ANA Pictures

9 *The forgotten heroes*

'What do you call a Maori on Prozac? Once were worriers.'

That was the intro to a front-page lead story in the *Cape Argus* that I now regret running. It was a crude reference to the film about Maori life in New Zealand, entitled *Once were Warriors*. Traditionally, newspapers have a lighter feel on a Friday, going into the weekend, and a major sporting event is usually a chance for the sports writers to make it onto the front page with a preview of sorts. The story was packaged under the headline, 'The Game that Splits a City'. It was all about how coloured rugby fans would support the visiting Crusaders team from New Zealand and not the hometown team, The Stormers, the following day at Newlands Rugby Stadium. It was 2011 and I was into my second year as an editor. I was young, brash and eager to make an impression. An issue that bugged me was that the Crusaders had a very vocal support base in Cape Town, dubbed the Cape Crusaders. The fans were predominantly coloured and most of them also supported the New Zealand national team, the All Blacks.

In hindsight, it was an editorial decision I now regret making and a story I now regret running. It was thoughtless, callous even, and I rode roughshod over the feelings of the very people most hurt by apartheid in sport.

At the time, I was angry at them for not getting behind our hometown heroes and instead backing a team from another nation in a now-democratic South Africa. My eyes would later be opened. There were many who grew up among this base of fans of New Zealand franchises and its national team who could have and should have represented their countries in various sporting codes, but were denied the opportunity due to the colour of their skin. There are thousands who never got the opportunity, despite being at the top of their game. They are the forgotten heroes.

One of them is a typically modest gentleman. If all things had been equal during his playing days, Vincent Barnes, or Vinnie as I call him, would've walked into the Proteas national team. Gentleman he may be, but he was a fierce competitor on the cricket field. Those who played with him were happy he was on their side. The batsmen who faced him showed him respect, as they bloody well should have. He was said to be as quick as Dale Steyn, but with the guile and cricketing brain of a Vernon Philander – all packaged into one unit.

Vinnie's exploits on the soccer field, especially for his beloved Battswood FC in Wynberg, are equally legendary. I watched him a few years ago, at William Herbert Sports Ground, as a 57-year-old, turning out for Battswood against a much younger team. Vinnie scored and had an assist that day. I'm 18 years younger, but Vinnie is in way better shape than I could even dream of being.

Yet, Vinnie isn't one to look back with regret. I thought it would be fun to write about what it takes to be an international cricketer when you're better than AB de Villiers, Virat Kohli and Kagiso Rabada, right? Wrong! When preparing to write the profile about Vinnie, I asked him for a trial in the nets at Newlands, to see if I had what it takes to be a Proteas player. Vinnie bowled an over at me that wasn't really at express pace. But he had me out with three consecutive balls. By ball four, I made contact with the bat with a poor, mis-timed shot. It was a mess. Vinnie had some harsh words for me when I told him I had prepared by eating KFC for breakfast – a team sponsor at the time.

When we sat down for the interview on the turf of the nets at Newlands Cricket Ground, Vinnie spoke in an animated way about how he loved his job of polishing the rough diamonds of the future – the Rabadas and Lungi Ngidis. He called it 'building the pipeline' - finding the new stars for our national team.

As assistant coach of the national team at the time, Vinnie played no small part in the Proteas reaching world number one in the Test and One Day International rankings. He accepted that he missed the boat as a player, but he was going to make damn sure he would make a difference as a coach and mentor – passing on his incredible skills and life experiences. Coach Vinnie and a few collaborators, like national academy coach Shukri Conrad and other domestic franchise coaches, have been filling the conveyor belt with new talent from all over the country. To understand his expertise, you have to know that

Vinnie was part of the national team set-up for eight years, first as an assistant coach and then a specialist bowling coach.

'I was actually a late starter in cricket. I loved the game, but I only started playing when I was about 13 years old. Adeeb Abrahams was my good buddy and took me with him to Victoria Cricket Club where he was playing,' he told me after showing me the many flaws with my batting technique that day.

'I joined and I always enjoyed bowling fast when we played cricket in the streets. I was quite naive at the time – I just wanted to bowl fast. I started playing in the under-14 side, then under-16. Then I was asked to play in the third side, then the second team; and by the end of the season I was playing in the first team as a 16-year-old.

'Cricket was a new thing, playing with a lot of the old boys. But I got insight from a lot of people who guided me along my career, and it helped grow my awareness. Playing as a club cricketer in the old board in the apartheid era, I just enjoyed it as a form of recreation. But I always wanted to be the best at what I was doing – whether it was playing football, cricket or darts, the competitive juices were always flowing. I played a friendly the other day and it was the same thing!'

But Vinnie was all too aware of the cruelty of apartheid South Africa as a schoolboy. 'I went to school at Livingstone High, which really opened my eyes politically to the situation the country was in at the time. Although sport was a major part of my life, I had to understand the context,' said Vinnie. 'I knew I was never going to play for my country, so I decided while playing a couple of years overseas to do all my coaching courses in England and went through all the levels. That was just to make sure, because I wanted to have a career in cricket, and I thought I wanted to make a difference to other people's careers.

'I played a couple of first-class games for Western Province and quite a number of Benson & Hedges one-day games here at Newlands. My love for coaching grew immensely. I started coaching at the age of 25. By the time of unity, I was well into my coaching. A few years later I was approached by Duncan Fletcher to apply for a position here, got it and never looked back since.'

Vinnie has worked with the best in the world – from Shaun Pollock, Makhaya Ntini, Dale Steyn, Morne Morkel and Charl Langeveldt to the current crop of players. While he is no longer involved in the national team set-up, many of them credit Vinnie as an integral part of their success. And his current role is perhaps even more important, as he does the groundwork for continued success by the Proteas by supplying a chain of exciting new players.

'It has been an unbelievable journey. You do travel to some fantastic places and you travel to some pretty average places. I wouldn't change it for anything,' he said.

'If somebody asked me, "What was the highlight of your coaching and playing career?", I'd say my whole life has been a highlight so far. I had the privilege of being involved with the Proteas for eight years and coached some of the most amazing fast bowlers, players, human beings – and my job still continues.'

On his surprise 60th birthday party, expertly arranged by his wife Debra Barnes, I was lucky enough to be in the audience as Vinnie reflected on his life in sport. He spoke candidly about his peers in the room: 'The group of guys in here made a promise to ensure that we would lay the foundation for the next generation. It was during the dark days of apartheid, that so many wonderfully, gifted, talented sportsmen like yourselves were denied the opportunity to represent your country, based purely on the colour of your skin.

'I've been fortunate that through cricket I could give back to the game I love so much – not in monetary value or recognition as a sports person, but through being gifted with the ability to identify talent and nurture that talent. I will continue to find and create opportunities for cricketers with talent, of which we have in abundance.'

In my humble opinion – as someone who failed my trial as a Proteas hopeful with Vinnie – Vinnie should have a shot as head coach of the national team. He has the experience and the eye for talent. He has life experience and knows all the conditions of playing surfaces around the world. You'll never hear Vinnie talk about it, as he is happy to serve. But he is the best man for the job – bar none.

A generation earlier, another sports phenomenon was driving over the apartheid roadblocks and making it in the then white man's world of motorsport – even though he didn't realise it at the time, because all he wanted to do was to drive as fast as he could. As my first Friday Files profile, I had the good fortune to sit down with Armien Levy to tell an untold story. I wondered why his story had never been told. A six-time champion of colour who tore up the then gravel track at Killarney. Given the chance, who knows, he could have represented South Africa in Formula One.

Despite being the champion at Killarney, he wasn't allowed to use the cafeteria and had to leave the venue when nature called because the white administrators wouldn't let Armien use the toilet. But Armien wouldn't let that deter him from becoming the best. In fact, it would make him even more determined. Now in his 70s, a corner display unit in Armien's home is covered with some 150 trophies from a successful motor racing career spanning five decades. But they don't tell the story of the adversity he faced.

In the tumultuous 1960s, Armien was single-minded about racing competitively, while working full-time as a motor mechanic.

'I went to Goodwood Showgrounds to watch stock car racing – that started my passion. A few of us came together and started our own club. We had cars, but we couldn't race. Nobody wanted to accept us because the laws of the time said coloureds, Indians and blacks were not allowed to compete in motorsport. But I wanted to do it. The leaders of our club, the Cape Daredevils, were political guys, so they didn't want to race. I applied so I could race under a permit; but they didn't want to.'

The authorities gave the Cape Daredevils a piece of land where Mitchells Plain is now. While it was free, it was deemed unsuitable by Armien and fellow club members, but Armien refused to give up. 'I was never a political person. I just wanted to live my life, and I wanted to race – that's all I wanted to do.'

Armien approached Jack Holloway of the Goodwood Show-grounds. 'He said to me: "Armien, I can help you guys. I can give you a date." He gave us the worst date of the year – 28 December (1969). Who's going to come to motorsport on the 28th of December?' Armien recalls. 'But I accepted it because it was better than nothing. Then he said to me, I'd have to come up with R2 000 for this, and R2 000 for that – the total bill was R6 000. In today's money, it was about R600 000. I went back to our committee and they rejected the proposal. 'Eventually, I spoke to the drivers outside of the meeting, in a caucus, and they said: "Armien, let's go for it".'

Armien went back to Holloway, who agreed to bankroll the race day – but it was going to be his show.

'For the first time in history, the authorities had to close the road at the robots on Voortrekker Road and at the fire station. No one could come in after 4.30pm – the place was already packed! My racing car was first at the gate, about four or five of us towing our cars – we couldn't afford trailers back then,' he remembered with a smile on his face.

'As we came to the gate, one of the officials asked where we were going, in Afrikaans. He said: "No, this isn't for *hotnots*.[14] You must turn around."

'But Holloway had given me two sheets of A4 paper – one was the proof of having a permit, and the other was the proof from the racetrack and the council that we could race here.

'But the official said: "You better *donner*[15] out of here now before I call the police."

'The police came, took our papers, scrunched them up, threw them in the bin and said, "F-off."

'Luckily, Holloway arrived on his motorbike and waved us through. Even with the permits and everything, they wanted to chase us away.'

Armien's face beamed with pride as he recounted the moment he drove his V8 stock car onto the gravel track of the circuit. 'When we got inside, I'm telling you – my very first race. Oh! There is not one moment that can overtake that feeling. Look at these goosebumps on my arm! Here I am on Goodwood Showgrounds.

'My admiration for the Sarel van der Merwes, the Deon de Waals and guys like that gave me that urge. If they can do it, I can also do it.

'I could hear the clapping, but no names. There was no hero yet among our people. These cars are very loud: exhausts by your ears, helmet on and you can hear nothing but the cheering of the crowd.

'The first race was a draw out of the hat, and I drew No. 1 – my luck – and I won that race. Then the crowd started roaring, "Armien Levy! Armien Levy!" The people were on their feet by now.

'For the second race, I drew third position. The officials told our officials that I must stand at the back. "He's too quick," they said. They made me go right around and, as I was going along the back straight, they let the other cars go. I could hear – through the noise, the concentration and the adrenaline pumping – the crowd chanting my name. I won that race as well. I never came second the whole night. It's there where I made my name, at Goodwood Showgrounds, and I became known as "Hell Driver – Armien Levy".'

But, instead of his successful debut being a launching pad for a career in racing, what followed was more humiliation. Levy applied for membership of the Western Province Motor Club. A response letter thanked him but reminded him that coloured people could not participate in motorsport. He was offered two tickets to the races at Killarney as consolation.

'I took the offer and went to Killarney,' he said. 'We couldn't go in through the main entrance, but between two trees was a rope, and this was the entrance for coloured people. I was the first one there to come to Killarney.[16] For me it was great, no matter where I stood, to see the racing.'

But, after he completed an international rally in which he performed well, the same Western Province Racing Club that had denied him membership claimed him as its own. There was a media scrum outside his house when he arrived back from the rally.

'So they came back and said to my father and his lawyer that they would allow me to race at Killarney. They would scrap the restrictions. I couldn't use their bathrooms and toilets or the cafeteria, and it was accompanied by a long letter saying, "You're driving a dangerous weapon," and I mustn't bump the white man's car,' said Armien.

'Eventually they bumped me. So, they gave me a R2 000 fine or three months or six months suspension from racing. My wages were R2 000 a month, so I took the suspension. It was done to kill me; that's the way it went.'

Armien knows that, despite all the roadblocks put in his way, he had what it takes to be world class. 'I have a lot of talent – I'm not praising myself – but I was quite amazed to see what I could do behind the steering wheel. To come in for the first time on to a gravel track with a V8 – and winning races, starting from the back. Then I went to Killarney, and I was champion six times.'

These days you'll find Armien, still a mechanic, hunched over the engine of a stock car or rally car in his garage, run under the Armien Levy Motorsport banner. The racing bug bit three of his five children. Sons Anwar and Ebrahim still race, and daughter Fuzlin took up the sport when she was growing up. To this day, the Levys still have roadblocks placed in their path by a largely male and white governing body at Killarney racetrack.

But the theory that talent runs in the blood really hit home when I saw Ebrahim's son in action, tearing up the karting circuit as a nine-year-old competing against boys much older than him. It happened purely by accident. Ebrahim had told me about his boy before, but I got the chance to see him race while I was attending the 40th birthday party of radio personality and artist representative Ian Bredenkamp, which was hosted at Killarney. From a balcony, I saw a junior kart race taking place and decided to cross the pedestrian bridge to take a closer look. There, I found Ebrahim beside his son, Reza Levy, getting his kart ready. Reza looked like a mini Formula 1 racer in his uniform and helmet. I was just in time to witness something that would blow me away. On that Saturday, almost five decades after Armien Levy's win, his grandson Reza emulated him to win his first ever Kart Race at the Killarney racetrack.

For Reza, it's a very different Killarney to the one that Armien experienced at the height of apartheid. I had met the shy boy the previous year when his dad Ebrahim, also an accomplished driver at Killarney, came to see me to discuss Reza's karting career. After listening to his story, the *Cape Argus* sponsored Reza's race suit, helmet, boots and gloves. It was most satisfying to see the Grade 2 boy from Bishops Prep win the cadet class race in the *Cape Argus*-sponsored gear. Watching Reza race was a treat. He took the lead with two laps to go and held his nerve and his racing line as his nearest competitor pushed him to the finish. That Saturday would prove to be Reza's big day, because a few minutes later he also won the Micro Maps race – a new event that saw the racers tackle the full Killarney circuit. But Reza had to settle for third after his bumper became dislodged when he collided with another kart during a warm-up lap. Because the bumper wasn't intact when he crossed the finish line, Reza incurred a 10-second penalty.

'The goal is to race overseas because that is where it's happening. I would like for Reza to be racing in Europe by the time he is 15,' said proud dad, Ebrahim.

Reza has since won numerous races and accolades. Proud granddad Armien said after that first win: 'Reza has a lot of potential and takes his racing very seriously. I watch him when he comes into the pits after each race and if he did not do well he actually cries. That means a lot to me and that's why I let Anwar coach him. But he is a fighter like his dad, Ebrahim.

'Motor racing is a tough sport and expensive, but Ebrahim and his wife Camila are both behind him and that is very good. You sometimes get one of the parents against motorsport, but not with Reza. Watch out for him in the future.'

A decade before Armien Levy first raced at Killarney, a young Indian man from Durban was creating problems for the apartheid government too – with his freakish golfing skills.

'As he lined up to strike the ball, the boy adjusted his body this way and that, emulating the more seasoned golfers he surreptitiously watched as they practised their swing on the golf course nearby,' writes author Maxine Case in the opening paragraph of the biography of Papwa Sewgolum. The boy she described was arguably the finest self-taught golfer to have ever played the game. He did not use a real golf club, but a walking-stick that his fisherman father fashioned from a tree branch. Case writes that Papwa would accompany his father to the beach near the Beachwood Country Club in Durban, which served as Papwa's training ground.

Although he was known as the man with the wrong grip, there was nothing wrong with the golf game of the first person of colour to win a provincial open in South Africa, beating the legendary Gary Player in the process. But like all sporting greats who were not white in apartheid South Africa, Papwa was denied the chance of reaching his full potential.

Oscar-nominated film producer, Rafiq Samsodien, has designs on telling the untold story of one of golf's greatest players. Rafiq has the calibre too. The short film, *Asad*, which he co-produced, about the plight of Somali refugees, earned an Academy Award nomination in 2013. Rafiq, who commissioned Papwa's biography, plans to turn his life story into a major feature film. When Rafiq tells the story of Papwa's first encounter with golf on the beach as a young boy, the images he conjures up leaves the listener with goosebumps.

'As a young kid, you go with your father wherever he goes on his little escapades. Now you can kind of picture this little kid with his father. Back in the day, dogs were taught to bark at non-white people. So, the father always used to have a stick to ward off the dogs. The back of the stick was shaped like a golf club,' said Rafiq.

'From a distance Papwa used to watch these people playing golf and he took some kind of liking to it. So, all these balls used to come off the course, from hackers like me. Every day this kid used to take the stick and he used to be able to whack the balls, try and find targets and try and get the distance. He used to whack this ball from the age of six years old to the age of nine – every day, from the beach to his home, home to the beach, he played wherever he went. It was him, the stick and the ball. And he started to become better and better at what he was doing.'

Papwa's father recognised a rare talent in his son and approached the country club to see if it would let Papwa work there to get his son as close to the game as possible. Papwa eventually became a caddie.

It was while working as a caddie that Papwa met Graham Wulff, the chemist and businessman who founded the beauty product company, Oil of Olay, as a gift to his wife. Wulff took an instant liking to the young man and also realised his genius. He often allowed Papwa to play with him in a four-ball at the club – a move that was against the laws of the day. Wulff became a type of father figure, especially after Papwa's father took ill and died. Later Wulff was instrumental in Papwa playing in tournaments abroad.

In 1959, Papwa beat Gary Player for the first time in a practice round at Northfield in the British Open.

'He gets to play on a level playing field and basically cleans up in the practice round. The fact that he gets arrested by the South African security police for being there, he arrives late, he still gets to play, but he doesn't win, doesn't make him less of a champion,' said Rafiq.

Papwa qualified to play in the French Open but missed it by a day because of the complications the South African security police were causing him. But he entered and won the Dutch Open later that year. He returned to South Africa a hero of non-white sport, but he still wasn't acknowledged as a real champion. In 1960 and 1964 he successfully defended his Dutch Open title.

But the turning point for Papwa, in more ways than one, was winning the Natal Open for the second time in 1965 and beating Gary Player. The story goes that Papwa had to accept the trophy outside in the rain because he wasn't allowed inside the clubhouse.

It was clear that Papwa had become too powerful a symbol of the sports boycott movement. At the peak of his power, the apartheid government banned him from participating in, or attending, any PGA tournaments in South Africa. His passport was taken away and he could no longer compete internationally. In effect, golf was taken away from Papwa and it systematically broke his spirit.

There are many such stories of forgotten heroes like Vinnie, Armien and Papwa. Many are still alive and they need to be celebrated. But many legends who were never acknowledged have passed on.

It was these rare interviews, and the insight gained into the lives of the sporting greats of yesteryear who were held back by an unjust world, that gave me a deep appreciation for the Cape Crusaders. It is no longer an issue for me. I understand why they still feel a stronger allegiance to the Crusaders and the All Blacks than to the Stormers and the Springboks. The fact of the matter is, it is the Stormers and the Springboks that need to make the hard yards.

The first thing the Crusaders or All Blacks do when they arrive in Cape Town is visit the communities who come out to support them – from the Bo-Kaap to Mitchells Plain. They interact with the fans in a way the Stormers and Springboks have only recently cottoned on to. In particular, Sonny Bill Williams, a devout Muslim, is a popular figure as he attends congregational Friday midday prayers, called Jumuah, with the community in Lansdowne.

But it is also the culture of humility one can admire in the New Zealand rugby culture and the influence of Maori tradition that I now feel embarrassed about mocking. During a terrorist attack at a mosque in Christchurch in 2018, it was the Haka – the Maori war cry performed before every New Zealand match – that brought the nation together. Celebrated rugby scribe and author, Mark Keohane, would tell me how, traditionally, after a win, the captain of the All Blacks team would clean the dressing room of the stadium they were playing at.

While the iconic Newlands Rugby Stadium is revered by many, it is a place of deep unhappiness for many who didn't get the chance, but who were good enough. These Cape Crusaders look up from the stands and see a stand named after Danie Craven – a rugby administrator who notoriously said that black people could not play rugby.

Newlands will be torn down in 2021 for financial reasons and because it doesn't comply with legislated safety standards. It is difficult to reach via public transport and is old and antiquated. Rugby will soon be played at the incredible new Cape Town Stadium and with the move comes an opportunity for the sport to make a clean break. And a chance to embrace the Cape Crusaders. Instead of mocking their past allegiances, let's welcome them as part of a new tradition of tolerance.

After all, it takes just one autograph from Siya Kolisi to break the chain and make the son or daughter of a Cape Crusader a Stormers and a Bok fan. However, let's respect the legacy and never forget the reason why some communities support the teams they do. It is more than just a game for them. In a way, it is for a similar reason, other than sport, that I support Orlando Pirates of Soweto, instead of any of the Cape Town football clubs in my hometown. But also because I was first introduced to the team by former Sunday Times editor and then mentor, Mondli Makhanya, as a 19-year-old intern reporter at *The Star*.

After more than two decades of being a fan and studying the history of the club, I realised that Pirates – along with Kaizer Chiefs – was one of the few sources of joy for a black majority that otherwise knew only oppression. For 90 minutes or so, when matches were played, the nation's masses could forget about their struggle against the government. It is part of the reason the Soweto Derby, between Pirates and Chiefs, is still ranked among football's greatest rivalries – played, most of the time anyway, with intensity but with respect for each other by both the teams and their thousands upon thousands of fans. Think about that the next time you look at a Cape Crusader with disdain. I still support the Stormers and the Springboks, but I have no qualms about a guy sitting next to me in the stand wearing a Crusaders or All Blacks shirt.

Perspective matters – even in sport. Instead of having our own warriors, these coloured and black legends of yesteryear were instead forced to be worriers for unjust reasons.

26 November 2016. The late Ahmed Kathrada, former Rivonia trialist who served life in prison with Nelson Mandela, spoke to Gasant Abarder on the eve of the 2nd anniversary of Mandela's death and on the day he received the freedom of the City of Cape Town from mayor Patricia de Lille. Photo: Cindy Waxa. ©*ANA Pictures*

10 *Coloured or too coy to be Khoi?*

'You're the hack with the grenade. Don't fuck it up!'

Those were the words my *Daily Voice* editor, Karl Brophy, used to say to me when he left the office for a meeting or was going on a trip abroad and left me in charge. As I mentioned before, Karl was a news genius by instinct. He was five steps ahead of everyone and took calculated risks that showed in the kind of newspaper sales and growth rarely seen in the South African context.

He trusted me. Full stop. He knew I had what it takes to make the right calls.

It seemed cool at the time, until this responsibility became official. In 2009, I was appointed the youngest ever editor of the *Cape Argus*, at 31. It was a daunting challenge. There were journalists in that newsroom who had way more experience than me. In at least two instances, there were two greybeards – the term news people use for the veterans with institutional memory – who were double my age.

There was the burden of proving to everyone that a now former tabloid hack could be a successful editor of a serious newspaper. But another burden, which I never mentioned to anyone, also weighed heavily. I was all too aware that I was only the third person of colour – or 'coloured' to be precise – after Moegsien Williams and Ivan Fynn, to hold this prestigious position in the more than 160 years since the paper first rolled off the presses.

It shouldn't have haunted me so much; but it did. I started questioning my own self-worth, when it was explained to me very carefully by the then Editor-in-Chief and the rest of the local management that it was all about staying in your lane. The fact that I was coloured – the label the apartheid government had foisted on me – was no accident. The Irish owners didn't really care, as long as the South African business was making money hand-over-fist for them, without any investment being made back into the local papers. (We didn't even have Wi-Fi in our newsrooms).

As part of my induction, I was shown a triangular diagram of the *Independent Newspapers'* reader segmentation. *The Cape Times* reader was at the top – meant to be a smaller, sophisticated and business-minded readership. This was a euphemism for white readers in the leafy suburbs, who were greenies and who didn't want to choke on their marmalade on toast while reading their morning paper and sipping their Earl Grey tea. They represented the head.

Next up, in the middle of the triangle, was the *Cape Argus* – the oldest paper in the group. It was the heart, I was told. It had a larger readership as an afternoon newspaper and was meant to cater to the lower to middle income Capetonian who put in an honest shift as a blue-collar worker. It was meant to include a bit more pop culture than the aloof *Cape Times* and would often lead with aspirational stories. *The Argus* reader, I was told, aspired to drive what the *Cape Times* reader was driving. The *Cape Argus* reader, essentially, was a coloured man or woman.

To put it in stark perspective, the day Michael Jackson died, I splashed the news all over the front page and recorded a record sale for the *Cape Argus*. The *Cape Times* had a tiny column on the pop icon's death running down the side of page 3.

The *Daily Voice* was everything below the waist. The catch-all, with its salacious stories and bare-breasted Page 3 girls. It was the bottom of the triangle, as it needed to have mass appeal. This meant it should have more readers than both the *Cape Argus* and the *Cape Times* – and it did under Karl's editorship. It was meant to be for the lower-income groups – less sophisticated and prone to soapie-style news and gossip stories.

But the *Daily Voice's* sales were starting to encroach on *Argus* sales. It was a hit – irreverent, yet a champion of the working class, with proper investigative and advocacy journalism. It was picking up on areas the *Argus* missed because of the blind spots defined along racial groups in the Western Cape. With Karl, and sometimes under the leadership of 'The hack with the grenade', we were telling stories that had universal appeal – whether you were black, white, gay, straight, coloured or a CEO of a large corporation. There was a running gag that businessmen in suits would be seen buying both the *Argus* and the *Daily Voice* and would tuck the latter inside the former – just to get a peek at the Page 3 girl of the day.

Later, the clever general manager at the time took a decision to remove the Page 3 girl and make the content of the *Daily Voice* more 'palatable'. Karl had long since moved on. It was decided that the *Daily Voice* would be pitched as a platform for advertisers, rather than a mass sale publication. This would hurt the *Argus* eventually, as the Pick 'n Pay and Checkers ad spend then had to be shared with the *Daily Voice*. It was self-inflicted cannibalism.

In that context, I became the *Cape Argus*' editor – a 'bolt out of the blue', as I was described by the Editor-in-Chief of the regional group of newspapers at the time. I was 'a bit of a gamble on a maverick'. I was all too aware of the initial chatter that I would turn the *Argus* into a tabloid, as I settled into my office and got used to having my own personal assistant, Lyntina Aimes. Lyntina is an amazing friend who helped me get me through those first few tough months.

I had serious self-doubt when I took on the job, but I knew I could do it and I was willing to learn. I had written for papers like the *Cape Argus*, *The Star* and the *Cape Times* and I knew the rhythms and the style. But there was my coloured self that was bothering me, along with the notion that I was a strategic placement along racial lines. In hindsight, the genesis of this self-loathing of my colouredness at that time took root in my time as a TV reporter at *eNews*.

In the early 2000s, when I was in my early 20s, I was head-hunted by arguably one of the best TV news minds in the business, Jimi Matthews. The guy was a visionary and believed that TV news should be about storytelling – the way it is meant to be told. I was in awe of the guy. I said to Jimi that I would love a job at *eNews*, but I was honest that I knew nothing about TV journalism. Jimi wasn't fazed at all and said that I was being hired because I was breaking stories in the *Cape Times* as the crime and court reporter. They would train me in all things TV news.

So, on day one I was assigned a story about the murder of a farm owner in Pniel whose wife was the prime suspect. Sports anchor and good friend Eben Jansen insisted on going along on the story to help me through it. And Lucky Tsolo – a cameraman I count as a great friend, as we would later make up the news team's two-person parliamentary team – was there filming the story. I was literally shaking as Eben made me do about 30 takes for a piece to camera. Lucky was very patient, while Eben was adamant that I would succeed and that I would do as many takes as I had to until he was happy.

That night the story went on air. I was excited as I watched the story with my family and there was a collective whoop when the piece to camera played out. At the same time, I was trying to disappear into my chair because I hated the sound of my own voice.

At first, I thought this TV news lark was easy. But I was wrong. After that first story, I was cock-a-hoop and was assigned a number of stories. But for weeks on end, my stories never made it to air. I was very young and too polite to ask why my stories weren't making the bulletins. Sometimes there would be a cameo in the 10pm news bulletin, thanks to then producer An Wentzel – but never in prime time.

Then I was informed I was to do training at the Voice Clinic, a place just down the road from the e.tv studios. This was to get rid of my sing-song delivery and to help me project my voice better. It helped immensely and soon I was reciting, 'Peter Piper picked a peck of pickled peppers. If Peter Piper picked a peck of pickled peppers, where are the pickled peppers Peter Piper picked?' I was advised that I should roll my Rs and breathe deeply from my diaphragm during the delivery of my script to help me project more effectively. I was put through my paces to improve my diction and encouraged to speak that way in my normal conversations with people off air – as if I was doing it for TV.

I was so young and naïve that what I didn't realise at the time was that, while my diction and delivery were improving and my stories were finally making it to air, my coloured accent had been beaten – or as we say, 'moered' – out of me. People I grew up with in Mitchells Plain, Salt River and Woodstock were wondering why I was 'putting on'[17] and being 'sturvy' – a colloquial word for being a snob or being aloof. My new broadcast voice had turned me into a *Cape Times* reader overnight!

But my confidence grew, and I was being trusted more and more with big stories because of my journalistic abilities. Eventually, I was reporting from Parliament as the sole correspondent, and Lucky and I would get through three stories a day. He somehow got Parliament's agenda, called the Order Paper, before anyone else, and would be tipped off about which briefings to attend and which would be a waste of time. He was an immense resource and an operator[18] – a journalist at work, even though his skill was video. We would regularly beat the SABC on stories, although the government broadcaster had far more resources and about a dozen journalists.

About a decade later, then older and more experienced, I had time to sit in my office and reflect back on those days. I realised then that radio and TV advertisements were using exaggerated coloured accents more and more to sell products. It made sense in a way, even though I found it patronising. The idea was that a coloured voice would appeal to a coloured audience. Hence, I was here now – at the *Cape Argus* – as my coloured self, sans my coloured accent. At least the readers couldn't hear me speak!

It made me think too. If you've ever watched an international news network, the reporting is authentic because a Scottish guy is reporting live from Scotland, an American is reporting live from America and an Australian is reporting live from Australia. The news broadcaster wouldn't dream of asking the correspondent to speak English with the Queen's accent, right?

The truth is, I had some clangers as front page leads in those first few weeks as the new *Cape Argus* editor, when I was really just a tabloid hack wearing a suit and tie. But slowly but surely, and conscious of my self-identity, I began to get into the *Cape Argus* rhythm and I stayed in my lane. I was assimilating. The *Cape Argus* reader was aspirational. They wanted to send their kids to good schools, drive nice cars and own houses in posh suburbs. That was why BMW, Apple and Pam Golding should be advertising.

Stick to your brief, Gasant – we're the paper for the blue-collar worker (shorthand for coloured people). I enjoyed the job. It was conventional and very conservative. Rules were rarely broken. I wouldn't have dreamt of allowing students to edit the newspaper during that first stint as editor.

Now I listen to talented coloured broadcast journalists on radio and TV who have maintained their identity. I know when I watch Monique Mortlock on eNCA – the 24-hour news channel that eNews later evolved into – that she is true to herself and knows where she comes from. She is a rising star in the business and doesn't roll her Rs. I can't imagine anyone telling her to change who she is.

One of my best friends, Robin Adams, a sports anchor who has worked at eNCA, Al-Jazeera and now TRTWorld in Turkey, doesn't roll his Rs either. He is proudly from Atlantis and tells everyone who cares to listen. Robin is a dynamic talent who can go pound for pound with the best sports broadcasters in the world. Yet, when you watch him do his thing, there is no doubt where he is from. He knows. It's in his smile and his confidence. It is something I wish I had back when I was a TV journo.

Yet, we still grapple with this coloured identity. Some accept it wholeheartedly, while others reject it with contempt as an apartheid construct. Others still, prefer to be referred to as Khoi or San. But for the most part, my personal feeling is there is a coyness about that too. I have borrowed from Eusebius McKaiser's definition in his book *Run, Racist, Run* and believe myself to be politically black, but culturally coloured. When I mentioned this to a black colleague while at an airport in Washington, he laughed in a derisive, contemptuous way.

While at the *Daily Voice*, I remember a splash a colleague wrote after the mayor's media advisor Blackman Ngoro referred to coloured people as drunks. He stated in a piece that 'coloured people were beggars, homeless and drunk on cheap wine'. He later apologised and admitted the words 'how vastly superior Africans are' were insulting and hate speech. He also admitted that saying 'coloureds have not yet realised that the time to be the cheerleaders for the white race is long past and gone…', was unjustified. The *Daily Voice* responded with a front page about what made coloured people great – complete with images of gatsbys[19], missing front teeth and being in the Klopse[20].

I was angry at both these incidents for a long time. I now look at the situation very differently. With maturity, one finds a way to self-define. I am coloured, but I am way more than the colour of my skin or the texture of my hair. I am the descendent of slaves who were stolen from their countries in the East.

My own investigations tracked my maternal great-grandfather to Batavia (which is now known as Jakarta, Indonesia) and my paternal great-grandfather was from India. When my paternal granddad, who was also Gasant Abarder, wanted to visit a Muslim shrine (called a kramat) on Robben Island, ahead of his pilgrimage to Mecca with my grandmother in the 1960s, he was quick on his feet when he responded, 'Cape Malay', to a police officer when asked what race he was. Coloured people weren't readily allowed to go to Robben Island. So, when Gasant Abarder (the 1st) said 'Cape Malay', the police officer was confused, but seconds later said, 'Okay, you can go.'

I suspect it was because of my granddad's cunning and wit that I have this uncommon slave surname of Abarder – said to be derived from the East. Other slaves weren't as lucky. When they arrived in the Cape, their oppressors gave them English surnames that were easier to pronounce than their given surnames. This is why there is a proliferation of coloured people with the surnames January, February, March, April or whatever month of the year they arrived in the Cape.

It is encouraging that organisations like the Iziko Museums have undertaken projects to help people like these, named after months of the year, to track their ancestry and to tell their stories.

I am a mixed masala of backgrounds. Sometimes, when I am confronted with official documents and I see the word 'coloured' as a box to tick, I wince. Not because I am ashamed to be coloured – not at all. But because I am so much more than this category that the apartheid oppressors gave me. Whenever I encounter those compulsory race category boxes we have to tick on official documents, I'm tempted to tick three boxes: coloured, Asian, black. But inevitably, because I know that is how the world sees me, I tick 'coloured'.

When I covered the Communist Party of China's congress in Beijing a few years ago, I travelled with a group of about 50 fellow African journalists. None of them looked like me. If you looked at them, they looked African. Soon, the friend I made from Zimbabwe was calling me Gupta – a joke about the Indian family at the heart of the 'state capture' that occurred during the Jacob Zuma presidency.[21]

The world's journalists had descended on Beijing to cover the conference – about 3 000 correspondents all told. There were more laughs among my African colleagues when a contingency from Bangladesh stopped me to ask where I was from. When I said South Africa, they laughed and said it wasn't possible. Because of the way I looked I had to be one of them – a Bangladeshi. They wanted to know why I didn't look like Mandela. I eventually had to show them my South African passport to convince them, and they shook their heads in disbelief. Some gave me a business card and asked me to make contact when I was back home. It was hilarious.

Colouredness was rammed home even more when former Springbok rugby player turned TV analyst, Ashwin Willemse, walked off the set of the *SuperSport* studio in 2018. The coloured identity was raised on my Twitter timeline in the wake of Ashwin's walkout. One Twitter user posted how proud she was of her coloured identity, while another said he hated the classification because it was one given to him by apartheid's architect, Hendrik Verwoerd. Then a few black tweeters asked what these people, who are defined by the law as coloured, should call themselves. Among black people there was disagreement too: some believe coloured people are black and others believe they're not.

As my friend Robin Adams so aptly puts it in situations like these, 'What can must happen now?'[22]

But am I entitled to tick all three of those boxes? Is it okay for me to be all these things? Firstly, I am proud of my coloured identity. I jol[23] with the klopse, eat gatsbys, speak in a special dialect when I'm with my own, and participate in many other practices that are unmistakably coloured. Secondly, I am a descendant of Asian slaves who were brought to Cape Town by Dutch oppressors. That part of my ancestry gave me my religious identity as a Muslim, and my family still uses words like tramakassie (thank you) from those days. To say I am exceptionally proud of this heritage would be an understatement, and I work hard to preserve it in my household. Thirdly, I am black. Well, I certainly am not white. I identify politically as black because I subscribe to the ideologies of Steve Biko and identify with the oppressed nations of black people here and all over the world. I have the same skin colour as most black people. But apartheid was so evil in its intent that it was designed to tear people's identities apart like this.

It has to be acknowledged that there were varying degrees of privilege under apartheid too – from no privilege for blacks, a few scraps of privilege for coloureds, and absolute privilege for whites. This deliberately created resentment and animosity between different groups that is still present in democratic South Africa two-and-a-half decades later.

Political parties, particularly here in the Western Cape, still exploit these racial tensions because they bank on voting blocs being defined by race groups. What have successive political parties and movements achieved in bringing coloured and black people together in Cape Town and the broader Western Cape? The sum total of nothing.

In Cape Town, Jakes Gerwel Drive separates Langa and Bonteheuwel. The people of these suburbs barely talk to each other. The same can be said for Gugulethu and Manenberg, which are divided by Duinefontein Road. So, too, for Khayelitsha and Mitchells Plain, which are divided by Spine Road.

It gets even worse when you leave the city and enter the rural towns of the Western Cape. It is the apartheid era's Group Areas Act in living colour – in 2020.

I listen to the words of one of the most gifted coloured lyricists of his generation to come from the Cape Flats. His name is Riyadh Roberts and he is perhaps the most important voice in the coloured community right now. He is better known to all as Youngsta CPT. I'm supposed to be too old to listen to his rap music, but I've had it on rotation in my car for almost a year now – to be played when the kids aren't with me because of the explicit lyrics. Expletives aside, his rap is raw and uncensored social commentary about life as a coloured person on the Cape Flats. His debut album, *3T – Things Take Time*, tells a narrative that celebrates the coloured identity, warts and all, and proudly so too. The brilliantly written and composed tracks on this full feature album barely received radio airplay, despite Riyadh winning awards for album of the year and rap artist of the year.

One Youngsta CPT song got radio time, *Young van Riebeeck* (a play on his own stage name and Jan van Riebeeck – colonialist-in-chief) struck a chord with me. The track and the music video illustrate this very young artist's astute observations on colonialism, racism and the lot of coloured people. The lyrics go like this:

'A lot of mense[24] is hating but that's not surprising
The hip-hop game is like a country I am colonising
This is my Call of Duty I'm not even pocket dialing
When I stiek uit,[25] it's like the British and the Dutch arriving

When they landed at the sea shore
And they thought the Cape was just a detour

'Educate yourself read more
Before they're signing your deceased forms
I can't tell you how this feels, yoh
This the city I would bleed for
But I'm at the bottom of the seesaw
Hoping praying for a beanstalk

'Cape Flats or Sandton, uh
I be lifting every sanction, uh
Since the segregation happened, uh
Why I feel like this is the anthem, uh
Sorry bru, you must be lost
Now you acting posh, you a fake boss
You've been brainwashed to the chaos
Same cut not the same cloth, uh

'Talking up to God a lot, on my knees I'm in the mosque
Taking Jan van Riebeek to the barbershop and cutting off his whole
moustache
He was worried about the waves, I was worried about the slaves
Now you standing there amazed
Go tell the mense what's my name

[Chorus]
'It's the Cape crusader
Young Van Riebeek
I put it down like
Young Van Riebeek
What the name is
Young Van Riebeek
Kaapstad[26] did it
Young Van Riebeek
Young Van Riebeek
Young Van Riebeek
(Chorus repeats)

'A lot of mense is hating, that's not stopping me
This was the same thing that they did in the Cape Colony
Making us think we living free in a broken democracy
But the truth will set us free, you'll read it in my biography
When they brought us on the slave ships
And they took away our education
Looking for an oasis
Coz they turn our people into vagrants

'You can't win with the racists, coz they still think with that hatred
But victory is my fragrance so I'm emphasising my statements
We was locked up in the ghetto, far away from the meadows
No Shakespeare, no Othello, what you hearing is a demo
Had to scream until it echoes, from Khayelitsha to Soweto

'Call me Stefano Dimera
You was shocked I turned into a pharaoh
But they got us in a system
Our history was rewritten, by the Europeans and Britain
We all share the same symptoms
But you can never ever hide the scars
Take a look at how far behind we are
Now come meet the man behind the bars, his initials are YVR'

His words are profound, in your face and in a language that young coloured people can relate to and identify with. Youngsta CPT is in demand and other artists are lining up to collaborate with him. He headlines most music festivals and performs at sold out gigs. He has his own clothing line and a brand that everyone wants a piece of. I love his confidence in his coloured identity. He is a modern-day genius.

Youngsta CPT gives people hope where there is little to go around. The coloured people of the Cape – who a former ANC hack once infamously said there was an over-concentration of in the Western Cape – have struggled to find their identity. Through his rap music, Youngsta CPT reminds us all of who we are and why we must never forget.

There is a saying among coloured people that laments the days of apartheid when they were 'too black'. Now they're too white. During the days of apartheid there were also light-skinned coloured people who had themselves successfully re-classified as white, and who enjoyed all the privileges that came with being white. Imagine how they are feeling right now.

These days I am comfortable in my skin. I love being coloured and Cape Malay, even though these labels are an apartheid construct. To me, being coloured means being able to speak gham – a dialect that Wikipedia describes as the language of 'uncivilised coloureds'. It means going around to the neighbours' houses, no matter their belief or faith, during Ramadan, or sending a plate of daltjies,[27] fritters or samoosas. It means playing kennetjie[28] in the street or sharing a huge gatsby with your friends, after each contributes a bit of cash. It means going to the Galaxy nightclub or waiting for the Cape Malay choirs on New Year's Eve. It means koesisters on a Sunday morning and waking up to have your face painted so you can take part in the minstrel parade on Tweede Nuwejaar.

Growing up coloured means being part of a community that shares. It means being taught how to stretch a rand. It means getting by with what you have and always having enough to go around. It means visitors dropping by unannounced and serving them refreshments made with diluted cold drink concentrate. It means laughing at yourself and the thousand memes out there about being coloured. But most of all, to me anyway, it means resilience.

I am fortunate enough to work as the media manager at the University of the Western Cape (UWC). UWC was conceived by the apartheid regime as a 'bush' college[29] for coloured people to qualify as nurses or teachers. The university's Senate Building is still intact, with the old benches where the old parliament of the Coloured Affairs,[30] used to sit. UWC wasn't open to any other race groups. But a defiant Jakes Gerwel (who later became President Mandela's Director General), as Rector and Vice-Chancellor, defied the government of the day and opened up UWC to all races. Sixty years later, UWC is now the biggest 'up yours'[31] to the apartheid regime, because it has by far transcended its original role of being a college for coloured civil servants who could never be scientists or physicists. It now offers chemical science, astrophysics and even a postgraduate qualification related to virtual reality. It has one of the most respected law faculties in the country, and the most scientists involved in the Square Kilometre Array (SKA) telescope project.[32]

UWC is ranked among the top universities in the world and has arguably the most representative student body in the country, with black, coloured, Indian and white students reflecting our nation's demographics. It is so organically and not deliberately. It has alumni all over the world and seeks solutions to the United Nations Sustainable Development Goals through global partnerships in research and innovation.

Every day, I thank my lucky stars that I work at a place where I can be myself. My own coloured identity is further enriched by my white Muslim spouse and my Christian in-laws. Yes, our children truly are coloured and multi-cultural, and subscribe to interfaith.

And really, is that such a bad thing?

I was wondering about Prince Harry when he married Meghan Markle and whether the royal family fully considered that the former Duke and Duchess of Sussex would have coloured children? Not long after, little Archie was born – and he is coloured, just like my kids. How is that for irony? And how lekker that makes me laugh!

During my journey and experiences in newsrooms over the past 21 years, and now as a communications professional, I have learnt that my diverse heritage is actually my strength. If all newsrooms realise this, they will enrich the diverse narratives of our country. I love my colouredness and I've embraced it. I'm as South African and African as any other South African or African.

You can pass the grenade to this hack any time. He knows what to do with it!

Notes about the author

Gasant Abarder is a journalist who has worked in print, radio and television newsrooms, in both Cape Town and Johannesburg, for 21 years. The second decade of his working career was spent in senior editorial roles – including as Deputy Editor of the *Daily Voice*, Editor of the *Cape Argus* for two stints, Editor of *Eyewitness News* in Cape Town and Editor of the *Cape Times*. The author was featured in the 2013 edition of the *Mail & Guardian's* prestigious Young South Africans 2013, has previously served as Deputy Chairperson of the South African National Editors' Forum, and was a weekly columnist for the *Weekend Argus*. He is currently employed as Media, Marketing and Communications Manager at the University of the Western Cape, and lives in Cape Town with his wife and children. This is his first book.

His life ambition is to become a Chicken Licken brand ambassador.

Endnotes

1   A common expression used in certain South African communities. The closest English equivalent is, 'whatever' (or literally 'crap'). It is used as a dismissive phrase.

2   Many people in South Africa are familiar with the traditional Afrikaans community's koeksister, which is twisted pastry with lashings of honey or syrup. The Cape Malay variant is koesisters. It is different, as it has naartjie peels and aniseed in the mix and is coated with coconut. The koesister is a fixture in most Cape Flats homes on a Sunday morning.

3   Literally 'Second New Year'. This is a tradition from the days when slaves had the day off on the day after New Year's Day, and spent it mocking their masters. The tradition has evolved into a famous carnival in Cape Town. Every year, on the 2nd of January, the minstrel descendents of slaves participate in a carnival of song and celebration wearing colourful costumes.

4   The word 'tik' is commonly used in certain areas of Cape Town to refer to crystal meth. The word is a reference to the ticking sound the crystals make when they are heated in a glass pipe.

5   This is a colloquial word for a small, basic dwelling – often a Wendy house or similar structure – erected in the back yard of a Council-let property. It is sub-let by the Council-house tenants.

6   These are harder and more addictive drugs.

7   Translated literally as 'shitting on your own veranda'. The meaning is 'not writing about things too close to home'.

8   This is a traditional festival with Cape minstrels marching in the city streets in Cape Town on the 2nd of January each year. It is a famous, colourful, music-filled festival that draws tourists from all over the world.

9   Bonita was saying that some people believed that Bonteheuwel was established after the District Six removal programme (or as a result of it). This touches on the sensitivity of this matter and that a lot of what happened all those years ago is not conveyed factually these days.

10 Note: Small grammatical corrections have been made to the Twitter thread items, for purposes of this book, as they would have been understood at the time, with the situation being reported in the media, and because they were written for Twitter, e.g. without articles, conjunctions, punctuation, etc. But the original statements may prove difficult to understand for the reader of this book.

11 It is closer to the media glare, as it is situated right under their noses, i.e. right next to the Cape Town CBD.

12 Afrikaans word for veranda. In common use in South Africa.

13 Afrikaans word for little girl.

14 This is a derogatory term for coloured people.
15 This translates from Afrikaans as: 'You better get the hell out of here'.
16 More correctly: I was among the first coloured people to come to Killarney.
17 A colloquial way of saying: 'putting on airs and graces'.
18 Colloquial way of saying: 'a classic newshound'.
19 An enormous Cape Flats-style sub sandwich with hot chips and polony or steak.
20 The Kaapse Klopse are the famous Cape minstrels who usher in the new year in a celebration of colourful, satin and sequin tuxedos while singing and playing music. This is a famous annual event in Cape Town.
21 In, arguably, one of democratic South Africa's biggest scandals, the media revealed how the Gupta brothers – who had something of a newspaper and TV news media empire – had a say in who became a cabinet minister in SA, and lined the pockets of the president – generously. This carried on for years and at the time this book was published, one lone public servant, who had allowed the Guptas to land a jet full of wedding guests at the SA Airforce's Waterkloof airforce base in Pretoria, was the only person to face any consequences: he was relieved of his duties. This was despite the promises that there would be prosecutions for the 'state capture' saga.
22 This is a deliberately contorted colloquial phrase that is used to express complete exasperation at a hopeless set of circumstances.
23 Colloquial Afrikaans way of saying 'dance'.
24 People.
25 Arrive.
26 Afrikaans version of Cape Town.
27 A fried savoury treat made from chickpea flour and also known as chilibites.
28 A Cape Flats game played with two bricks, a stick and what looks like the bails of a cricket set.
29 So termed because it was literally situated in the bush (wild natural area) which is now the Cape Flats Nature Reserve.
30 The legislators who passed laws specifically for people classified as belonging to the coloured community
31 A colloquial way of 'thumbing the nose'.
32 On its website, the university states that the SKA, located in the Karoo in the Northern Cape, 'is powerful enough to sense radio waves from objects millions or even billions of light years away from earth…the SKA telescope will allow scientists to look further back into the history of the universe than ever before, and will give much more detail on how the universe has evolved over the last 14 billion years, and how the stars, galaxies and galaxy clusters have formed and changed since the universe was young.' Being part of this project is a massive feather in the cap for SA and for this university.

Index

Illustrations indicated by page numbers in italics.